Helping Your Child Succeed After Divorce

Florence Bienenfeld, Ph.D., first attended California State University, Los Angeles, where she received a B.A. in education. Her early years as a teacher were formative for her understanding of the feelings and needs of children. In 1968, she received a degree in Special Education from the University of California, Los Angeles, and went into private clinical practice as an educational therapist. In 1974 she joined the Conciliation Court of Los Angeles County as a Senior Family Mediator/Counselor. She received her doctorate in Marriage and Family Counseling in 1981 from Columbia Pacific University.

Through her six years of private practice and her eleven years at the Conciliation Court, Dr. Bienenfeld developed a deep insight into the dynamics of the family and the impact of divorce on children, and a strong faith in mediation and the conciliation process. She has published numerous articles in professional journals, and has written two highly regarded books dealing with the subject of divorce: *My Mom and Dad are Getting A Divorce* and *Child Custody Mediation: Techniques for Counselors, Attorneys and Parents*. For three years she wrote a weekly newspaper column, "For Better or Worse" in the Santa Monica *Independent Journal*. Besides being a prolific writer, she is a much-sought-after lecturer, and has often appeared on television and radio.

Dr. Bienenfeld has been the recipient of two awards for outstanding service to families and children of divorce from the Association of Family Conciliation Courts, an international organization of judges, counselors and attorneys; she also received awards from the Mayor of Santa Monica and Los Angeles Councilwoman Pat Russell for outstanding service to the Los Angeles County Conciliation Court.

With her husband of thirty-five years, Dr. Bienenfeld lives in Pacific Palisades, California, where she continues to practice and write. They have three children and a growing number of grandchildren.

". . . It was over a year after my ex took my daughter away out of the country—and over two years since I had fled the country with both children—that Dr. Bienenfeld's name began to crop up. She was mentioned by the Single Parent Family Support Group at Family Services, where my son and I attended meetings. They all encouraged me to contact her.

It was an immediate relief to find someone who didn't take either my side, or my ex's—but who unrelentingly represented the needs of the children. I'll never forget the moment when my daughter walked into my arms after nearly one and a half years. I don't believe it would have happened without mediation. Maybe more violence. Maybe ongoing strife. But not the delicate, complicated, but workable bridge that we built, step by step, to cross over international barriers and a history of violence, kidnapping and vengeance. I felt such gratitude to our mediator at that moment as I've felt toward very few people in my life. I would recommend mediation to all parents who are considering divorce or separation and who have children.

The reunion required a strong act of trust from both of us— threatened as we were by past memories of vengeance and present possible betrayal. The leaps of faith we made— especially my ex—were only made possible by the trust Dr. Bienenfeld had created in both of us.

Since that reunion, several years have passed; slowly but surely we have achieved a more stable and trusting relationship, allowing us to cooperate in taking care of the children's needs in an increasingly mature, orderly, and responsible fashion. There are constant challenges, but I have hope and faith that we will continue to meet them."

—Name Withheld—

"Getting a divorce when you have young children feels like being thrown into the sea. Your first thought is survival and it's hard to think about what is best for anyone else. Looking back now, I thank God for Florence's presence during the mediation session. She was like a life raft. She helped us both get out of our feelings about each other and concentrate on what we could do for our kids."

—*A. M., Los Angeles, CA*

"Mediation is a crucial alternative needed to provide a sane and caring example to our children. Within the last ten years, our family has experienced both mediation and the adversarial approach. Clearly, mediation is the alternative preferred by the children. As our family has certainly suffered from the adversarial situation, I whole-heartedly recommend the constructive interaction advocated by Dr. Bienenfeld, guiding all of us into a more loving relationship with our children."

—*Dr. Arlene K. Magnus, Management Consultant, Los Angeles, CA*

"In a 1987 mediation in Los Angeles, I requested Dr. Bienenfeld to co-mediate a seemingly irreconcilable custody issue. Both parents were entrenched in their positions and court proceedings seemed inevitable. Using her mediation skills, background and training in child development, and sensitive explanation of the children's pictures such as those in this book, Dr. Bienenfeld literally transformed the parents into collaborative, caring problem-solvers who negotiated a workable compromise that put the children's needs first and even improved their parental communication. As a professional colleague, Dr. Bienenfeld has earned my respect and admiration for her skills as a mediator and significant contributor to our professional literature."

—*Forest F. Mosten, Family Law Attorney and Mediator, Los Angeles, CA*

Other Books by Florence Bienenfeld

*MY MOM AND DAD ARE GETTING A DIVORCE
(1980)*

*CHILD CUSTODY MEDIATION: TECHNIQUES FOR
COUNSELORS, ATTORNEYS AND PARENTS (1983)*

THE VEGETARIAN GOURMET (1987)
(with Mickey Bienenfeld)

HELPING YOUR CHILD SUCCEED AFTER DIVORCE

Florence Bienenfeld, Ph.D.

Hunter House

> Hunter House Inc.
> P.O. Box 847
> Claremont, CA 91711.

Grateful acknowledgment is given for permission to reprint copyrighted material from:

My Mom and Dad are Getting a Divorce, © 1980 EMC Corporation

Library of Congress Cataloging-in-Publication Data:

Bienenfeld, Florence.
Helping your child succeed after divorce.

Bibliography: p.202
Includes index.
1. Children of divorced parents—United States. 2. Parent and child—United States. 3. Divorce—United States.
I. Title
HQ834.B52   1987   306.8'9   87-21399
ISBN 0-89793-041-X

Book and cover design by Qalagraphia
Copy editing by Elizabeth Bartelme
Production editor: Jennifer D. Trzyna
Production and line art: Paul J. Frindt
Set in 11 on 13 point Baskerville by Highpoint Type & Graphics, Inc.
Manufactured in the United States of America
9 8 7 6 5 4 3 2   First edition

Contents

To the many millions of children of divorce who look
to their parents for care, guidance, reassurance,
comfort, and love;
and
To their parents, who in spite of their own anger,
anguish, and pain must nurture, protect, and help
their children to succeed after divorce.

Foreword

Dr. Florence Bienenfeld's latest book, written for parents of divorce, is a remarkable, well-coordinated contribution to the field of postdivorce counseling, mediation, and therapy. Dr. Bienenfeld's years of experience with children and parents of divorce are reflected in her poignant and sensitive understanding and portrayal of the pain and anguish experienced by children and their parents going through divorce and postdivorce critical transitions.

This book should have major impact upon mental health professionals, attorneys, mediators, and judges. I hope that it reaches a large number of these professionals, who come face to face with the war-torn child and adult victims of poorly handled separation and divorce.

The clinical examples given by Dr. Bienenfeld are precise and very much alive. They are appropriately shocking when they point to some very destructive attitudes that parents communicate to children as a result of their own pain and suffering. At other times, they display the chaotic world of children of divorce, who are caught up in custody wars. Throughout, Dr. Bienenfeld keeps a down-to-earth, direct, and honest approach which puts the examples in perspective. The children's drawings she has included in this book, along with relevant familial data, bring to life the inner turmoil and suffering of these children more effectively than anything I have seen before in print.

Dr. Bienenfeld's book points out the critical value of early intervention in helping parents achieve some measure of cooperation immediately after separation. She stresses the need for the parents to get off to a "good start" in an effort to avoid "the battles that may never end."

Dr. Bienenfeld addresses the most frequent battle issues in custody wars, using the format of answers to letters from distraught parents. She covers every possible dilemma and pitfall in child custody arrangements, with practical approach and advice for situations ranging from what to say and how to handle: feared sexual abuse; conflicts with grandparents; holiday schedules; great geographical distance between parents; concern over a gay parent; anxieties over a stepparent or other significant man or woman in the other parent's life. Her insightful responses to some of these universal and ofttimes very delicate perplexities in divorced families center on bringing significant structure and order into the shattered world of children of divorce. Her advice aims at developing a sense of security and an organized life pattern for the children. She points out how structure, security, and ongoing meaningful contact with both parents can replace fear, turmoil, and depression.

Dr. Bienenfeld's book includes an excellent description of how mediation can and does work. Her vivid descriptions of actual mediation cases again underline how she keeps the process focused on the needs of the children, and demonstrates how she includes children in the mediation process.

Congratulations to Dr. Bienenfeld for what I consider to be a masterpiece in the critical area of divorce and custody. Dr. Bienenfeld's book should establish once and for all that children of divorce need frequent and ongoing contact with both parents. And while reinforcing her emphasis, I would like to add that parents as well as professionals in our field need frequent and ongoing contact with Dr. Florence Bienenfeld's very fine book.

FRANK S. WILLIAMS, M.D.

Frank S. Williams, M.D. is the Director of Family and Child Psychiatry at Cedars-Sinai Medical Center in Los Angeles, and is a member of the California State Bar Association Standing Committee on Child Custody and Visitation. Dr. Williams and his mental health staff are considered leading experts in custody evaluations, and regularly consult to the L.A. County Family Law Conciliation Court.

Preface

If I were to ask your child what he or she wants to see happen after divorce, most likely your child would answer, "I want my mom and dad to get back together again, but if they can't, at least I wish they could be friends."

In sharp contrast to this, if I were to ask divorcing parents the same question, most would answer that he or she want to have nothing at all to do with the other parent.

How children do in life after a divorce depends to a large degree on how their parents behave and on the parents' attitudes toward each other.

Although each divorce and custody situation is unique, there are common problems and concerns that face many of you and your children. The family situations I describe here are true. I have changed names and other identifying material to preserve confidentiality, but every case actually happened.

The purpose of my book is to help you, the divorcing parent, create a safe and nurturing environment for your children after divorce. Only then can your children recover and heal, then blossom and succeed. The practical information, concepts, insights, examples, and suggestions contained in the book can serve as a guide to raising successful and happy children after divorce. This result is within your reach. How you can achieve this goal is the theme and content of my book.

You have my empathy, warmest regards, and best wishes. This is a very difficult period for you personally, and it will take you time to recover and heal yourself. But remember, what you do to help your children today will help create a brighter tomorrow for them—and for you.

Florence Bienenfeld
California, 1987

Acknowledgments

I wish to express my appreciation to Frank S. Williams, M.D., for reviewing my book and for his thoughtful foreword.

I would also like to thank Hugh McIsaac, Director of Family Court Services/Conciliation Court of Los Angeles County; and E. Ronald Hulbert, Ph.D., Psychologist and Supervisor of Training, Research and Staff Development, Family Court Services, Los Angeles County Superior Court, for reviewing and endorsing this book.

A special acknowledgment to Isolina Ricci, Ph.D., former Executive Director of the New Family Center in Palo Alto, California, and now Coordinator of Family Court Services for the State of California. Her pioneering work since the early 1970s, and her book, *Mom's House/Dad's House*, have greatly influenced the thinking, attitudes, and even the language of parenting after divorce.

I wish to thank the following people for their encouragement, endorsement, and support of my "Children's Drawings of Divorce" project: Stan Cohen, Ph.D., Executive Director, Association of Family Conciliation Courts, Associate Professor, Department of Psychiatry, School of Medicine, University of Oregon; Linda Damon, Ph.D., Director, Family Stress Project, San Fernando Child Guidance Center, Northridge, California; Meyer Elkin, MSW, former Director, Conciliation Court of Los Angeles County, Publications Director, Association of Family Conciliation Courts; William Felstiner, Ph.D., Director of Social Research, Institute for Civil Justice, Rand Corporation, Santa Monica, California; Jay Folberg, Professor of Law, Northwestern School of Law, Lewis and Clark College, Portland, Oregon; Judge Nancy Ann Holman, Superior Court, Seattle, Washington; E. Ronald Hulbert, Ph.D., Principal Family

Mediator/Counselor, Conciliation Court of Los Angeles County; Hugh McIsaac, MSW, Director, Conciliation Court of Los Angeles County; Professor Lawrence Hyde, former Executive Director, Association of Family Conciliation Courts, Nova University Law Center, Fort Lauderdale, Florida; Judge Richard A. Lavine, former Supervising Judge, Family Law Department, Superior Court of Los Angeles County; Meda Rebecca, Ph.D., Developmental Psychologist, Core Faculty, California School of Professional Psychology; Carl A. Whitaker, M.D., Professor of Psychiatry, University of Wisconsin-Madison; and the entire Conciliation Court of Los Angeles staff.

I also wish to thank the following very special friends and colleagues for their interest and encouragement: Joan Lachkar, Ph.D.; Arlene Karp-Magnus, Ph.D.; Forest F. Mosten, Family Law Attorney and Mediator; Ciji Ware, KABC commentator; and Rebeca Willis, M.F.C.C.

I wish to express my gratitude to my excellent typist and friend, Kay Neves, who makes it easy for me to be a writer.

A very special word of appreciation is offered to the thousands of parents and children I have counseled, along with my best wishes to them all.

Last but not least I wish to acknowledge and thank my loving and caring husband, Mickey; our three wonderful grown children and their spouses; and our growing number of adorable grandchildren, all of whom bring me such warmth and joy.

1

Introduction: Making Wise Decisions

When a boat is sinking, all the passengers are given life preservers. When a marriage comes to an end, a similar state of emergency exists, but no one hands you a life preserver. You, your children, and the other parent are on your own, thrashing about, trying hard to survive. Many parents in this situation feel like helpless, frightened children themselves, wishing someone or something would save them.

Imagine, then, how devastated and powerless children feel. A separation and divorce is a shocking experience for them, for their very existence depends on their parents. They sustain tremendous losses and experience great pain before, during, and after divorce. The crisis and tragedy of divorce is that this time, when parents are usually least able to help or even think about helping, is when children need their help most of all. In fact, if your child is to succeed after divorce, he or she will need your *utmost* help.

What I mean by the term "to succeed" is to turn out well, prosper, accomplish, thrive, and flourish. A child needs to make a good recovery from the trauma of divorce to do well in school, be happy, relaxed, and satisfied, and have a strong sense of self as well as a good self-image. Most important, the child needs to be able to love, to have good relationships, and eventually to be able to sustain positive intimate relationships in adulthood.

In order to help children achieve this success, divorcing parents must make wise decisions jointly at a time when it is extremely difficult for them to communicate or cooperate with one another. Many parents are so upset and in so much pain themselves that they are not willing or able to focus on what their children need. Without realizing it, they hurt their own children unmercifully.

The purpose of my book is to help parents create a nurturing environment for their children in spite of their own pain, so that their children will recover from the divorce, heal, and feel good about themselves and their lives. To accomplish this I offer encouragement, information, knowledge, and practical ideas that can help parents minimize the stress, pain, and loss for their children. The three ways to do this are by developing a closer relationship with the child, relating more positively to the other parent, and sharing parenting after divorce. Specific examples given in this book will help divorcing parents develop a suitable parenting plan, avoid hassles and arguments, and settle disagreements. I have also provided examples and guidelines for handling many situations that commonly come up in divorcing families, such as dealing with emergencies, deciding when your child needs outside help, and finding ways to settle disputes when parenting practices differ.

If the parents are in too much pain to work these issues out on their own, mediation can and should be used to help resolve conflicts. Resources for finding help of various kinds have been included in Chapter 9, *Where Help Can Be Found*, from lists of family and conciliation courts and mediation services throughout the United States, to a suggested reading list of books written for divorcing parents and their children.

Use this book as a practical guide and refer to it again and again. At a time like this, you and your child(ren) need all the help and support you can get. No matter how difficult, strained, or miserable your relationship with the other parent has been in the past, it is not too late to begin working together to help your children. Their emotional and physical health lie in your hands. If children are unhappy as children, it is unlikely that they will be happy as adults. It is up to you parents to protect them from unnecessary pain and to create a secure and nurturing environment for them. Children need parental cooperation and all the love they can get from both of their parents, and from their grandparents, stepparents, relatives, and friends.

If you free your child from parental conflict and allow him or her to enjoy a close and loving relationship with both parents, you will be giving your child a stronger possibility of happiness. This is by far the best gift you can give him or her, and by far the best way you can show your love.

Children learn about life from their experiences with their parents, and from the way parents behave and get along with one another. Children tend to repeat patterns they are familiar with, even when those patterns are destructive, and in this way behaviors are passed on from one generation to another.

Over a ten-year period as Senior Family Mediator/Counselor for the Conciliation Court of Los Angeles County, and for an additional ten years as a marriage, family, and child counselor in private practice, I have counseled thousands of divorcing parents and their children. Mothers and fathers have tearfully told me about their own pain and problems, their anguish, concerns, frustrations, anger, bitterness, disappointment, mistrust, and fears. They have discussed their thoughts, beliefs, and attitudes, as well as their desires and dreams for their children.

Most parents mean well, but some of them feel too threatened and too blinded by their own pain to think clearly and to make wise decisions regarding their children. Many are themselves struggling to work through their own painful childhood experiences and do not see how they are sentencing their children to repeat the same behaviors when they grow up.

The Pain of Divorce

Children's devastation

Difficult as a divorce is for parents, it is truly devastating for children, since they are completely dependent on their parents. In some ways it strikes them deeper. Often, they do not know what is happening and the guessing and uncertainty create traumas that may surface and demand attention much later in life. Many children never get to voice their pain, anger and frustration in the way their parents do. As a result, they tend to feel extremely helpless, isolated and confused. Still, children are remarkably resilient. Although they experience great pain and feelings of loss, most children can and will recover if their parents allow them to heal.

For many children, the greater pain comes *after* the divorce. Approximately one-third of the children of divorce lose contact with one of their parents, and untold numbers of children are tormented by the conflict as parents continue to argue and fight long after the divorce is final. Frequently, the children become the focal point for the arguments and bitterness. Parental hostility often escalates through the years, causing needless pain and suffering all around, and for some children there is just no relief.

What this does to children psychologically is not hard to imagine. The longer the parental conflict continues and the greater the tension, the greater the likelihood that serious psychological damage will result. In order to avoid feeling intense pain, some children protect themselves by turning off their feelings. The result is that they do not feel the pain anymore, but neither do they feel any other emotions, not even pleasant ones. In short, they turn into emotional zombies.

If they are continually exposed to intense pain and loss, children tend to experience negative feelings about themselves, about others, and about life in general. They become reluctant to risk loving other people for fear of being hurt again, and these negative attitudes work against happy and satisfying lives.

According to Drs. Judith Wallerstein and Joan B. Kelly, who conducted a ten-year study of children of divorce, if children are deprived of one of their parents, or if the parents quarrel and compete with each other, children tend to have lower self-esteem. Psychological damage will result and children may develop serious symptoms. These include anxiety, depression, regression, sleep disturbances including nightmares and sleepwalking, asthma, allergies, bedwetting, tantrums and tics. They may also grind their teeth, vomit, become clinging or overaggressive, begin daydreaming, or withdraw from relationships. Overeating or loss of appetite, poor school performance, delinquent behavior, self-destructive behavior, alcohol or drug abuse, frequent crying or absence of emotion, and difficulty in communicating feelings are other symptoms. Professional counseling should be sought if any of these symptoms persist.

It is not uncommon for parents to get off to a bad start at the separation and get locked into a negative way of regarding each other. They may try to get even with each other and punish each other for their pain. They may feel hurt and wounded, refusing to work together to help their children. When one parent tries to punish the other, it is the child who is punished and hurt most of all. Even when parents are upset and in pain themselves, it is essential that they consider their children, for children are very needy. They should not be kept waiting until parents finally get their lives together. They need at least a tolerable situation in which they can recover from the divorce.

Hundreds of thousands of children in the United States are involved in custody battles each year. They become victims of a legal system that promotes competition rather than cooperation between parents. Warring parents go into court trying to "win" their children, and during the battle children are often pressured to take sides or asked to choose where they want to live. This puts them in a no-win situation.

Battles over child custody tend to increase hostility between parents, thus lessening the possibility of later cooperation. Some battles continue for many years and children suffer tremendously. One sixteen-year-old boy, whose parents had been in court every year since he was six, told me, "I'm so disgusted that I have lost all my feeling for my parents." A twenty-one-year-old woman, whose parents divorced when she was twelve, said, "I remember freaking out in the judge's chambers when he asked me who I wanted to live with. I told him I wanted to live with my dad because my mother was moving away and

I didn't want to leave my friends. It made me feel terrible to have to choose, but everything is fine now, except that I have a terrible attitude about marriage. I don't think that will ever change."

The Mediation Process

Divorce mediation is a way of avoiding all of this. This powerful process can help parents resolve their problems out of court; moreover, it gives parents the power to make their own decisions, instead of having a judge make them. Child custody mediation offers parents the opportunity to meet with a trained, neutral third party (mediator), who helps them discuss the issues, their concerns and their differences in a neutral, nonadversarial setting. They are helped to focus on their children's needs and on the present instead of the past, and explore various alternatives for resolving their differences. When they are able to reach an agreement, the mediator assists the parents in writing it up so that it can later be made into a legal and binding court order.

Since January of 1981, mediation has been made mandatory in California when parents are litigating over child custody and/or visitation issues. This is to attempt to reduce the hostility between parents and effect a more positive outcome for the children. Reports indicate that it has been very successful in doing that and because I believe very strongly in the mediation process, I will give here a brief description of how I use it.

I see both parents together. After I explain the purpose of mediation, I structure the interview so that each parent has a chance to tell me how he or she sees the situation and what he or she wants to see happen. I encourage parents to talk about their concerns, feelings, and needs. Then I spend a few moments putting what they have said into perspective for them, and educating them about the needs of children in general and the developmental needs of their children in particular. I try to make communication between parents easier, and I assist them in discussing issues, focusing on their children's needs and looking at a range of alternatives. When parents are willing, I help them draft a parenting agreement that can meet their children's needs and the family's needs as a whole. If attorneys have accompanied the parents, they are included at the beginning and at the end of the session.

During the mediation process, much of my time is spent interviewing children and counseling entire families. My experience has been that children benefit tremendously from being included in the mediation process. The difference in the children's faces, attitudes, voices, and body language from the time they first walk into my office to the time they leave is observable and dramatic.

Some parents and professionals believe it is best not to include children in the mediation process because they might become upset, but these children are usually upset already. They often have no neutral person to talk to about their feelings, and many children carry feelings of loss, sadness, and frustration over into adulthood.

Including children in the mediation process gives them an opportunity to speak, to be heard, and to gain perspective about the difficult situation in which they find themselves. Most children leave the mediation session *less* burdened and better fortified for whatever may happen to them.

It also gives parents an opportunity to hear and see how much anguish their competition causes children. Some parents are then able to focus more strongly on their children's needs and less on their own positions, and are more apt to cooperate with one another in negotiating a suitable parenting agreement.

Even when children are not included in the mediation process directly, they benefit tremendously from the help and education given to their parents. The intervention often comes at a time when adults are too upset to deal clearly with all the different needs and demands of the situation. Sometimes I think of the work I do as making order out of chaos. It is most satisfying work.

At the present time, throughout the United States, mediators in conciliation courts and family courts, in private practice and in private mediation centers, are doing child custody mediation. It has proven to be not only cost-effective but also highly useful in helping families resolve disputes over children at any stage of divorce proceedings. Even though I have worked with thousands of families, I am still truly amazed as I watch seemingly impossible child custody conflicts being transformed through mediation.

One key to helping parents settle their differences is having sufficient time to work with them. It is essential that both parents have the chance to be heard, and that sufficient time be allowed to discuss the situation fully and to explore all feasible alternatives. Occasionally, follow-up phone calls or seeing each parent alone can have positive results. Quite often, when there is a stalemate, I find that including the children and providing feedback to the parents helps them to recognize their children's needs and thus reach an agreement.

In order to make a child custody agreement into an enforceable and binding legal document, it must be written up, be signed by both parents as well as by a family law judge or commissioner, and a stamped copy filed with the court. Once filed it becomes a court order, and should a parent refuse to comply with the order, the other parent has legal recourse and may file contempt charges against that parent.

Before matters escalate to this point, parents have the opportunity of airing their grievances to a court mediator or private mediator. At that time parents can talk to each other about their difficulties and can modify their agreement, if they are able to agree on the changes to be made. Considering the difficulty of the divorce mediation cases I see, it is amazing that an agreement rate of more than 70 percent has been possible. These agreements tend to hold up over time, and most of these parents do not return to court unless new problems arise.

The best possible result from mediation is that parents reach a suitable agreement regarding how they will parent their child after divorce. Ideally, their plan must meet their child's specific needs and make sense for all concerned. However, even when parents do not reach an agreement, the mediation process has usually encouraged them to focus on their children's needs and has exposed them to insights and alternatives they may consider in the future. Creating a better outcome for the children is the whole purpose of mediation.

Parenting After Divorce

Much of the anger and futility experienced by adults after a divorce stem from what happened during the marriage or events that took place at the time of separation. For many individuals the months just prior to and after separation are an extremely difficult time. Emotions are raw, and parents tend to blame each other for the breakup. During these stormy periods, parents sometimes do and say terrible things to each other, often quite oblivious to the pain this is causing their children. It is difficult for many men and women to separate "husband-wife" issues from "mother-father" issues. They do not realize that although divorce ends their marriage, it does not end their parental relationship.

Young children do not understand adult problems. They do not know what happened or why one parent has left. They are confused and bewildered, and sometimes believe that the parent who stays loves them more than the one who has gone. In reality, the one who leaves may have been ordered to go and be truly miserable about being away from them.

Children take divorce very hard, for they are extremely attached to both parents and most children want their parents to stay together. When parents separate, it knocks the props right out from under their children. It has been observed that children, as well as adults, go through a classic mourning process after divorce, much as if someone close to them died. First they experience disbelief, then anxiety, anger, sadness and depression, and eventually, if given reassurance, acceptance of the divorce and healing. This process can take a year or more. If they are ever to recover, feel secure, and succeed after divorce, they need to be told, to believe, and to feel that their mother and father both still love them and have every intention of continuing to take care of them, even though they now live apart.

No matter what has gone on between the parents, children still have a strong need to look up to both of them and maintain a good relationship with each of them. It is unfair to use children as pawns to hurt the other parent or to engage in a tug-of-war, pulling a child this way and that. In this war, children are the ones who are torn apart.

Children need frequent and ongoing contact with both parents, who must be willing to put aside their own hurt and anger and cooperate in setting up a workable parenting schedule. Frequent and regular contact with both parents can make children feel secure and prevent them from thinking they have been rejected and abandoned.

Most of all, children desperately need parental cooperation after divorce. They need two parents who are willing to work together as partners, even if they do not like each other or are not friends. Parents should take to heart and follow these six principles:

1. Stop blaming the other parent or yourself for what happened in the past. Realize that the past is behind you and cannot be relived.

2. Realize that your child needs *two* parents. Be willing to share your child with the other parent.

3. In your discussions with the other parent, stick to issues pertaining to your child. Do not bring up other matters.

4. Stay focused on your child's needs today and from now on.

5. Work together with the other parent to provide your child with as safe and as conflict-free an environment as possible.

6. Make every effort to be civil to your former spouse, and defuse tension and animosity so that your child can have a decent, peaceful, and satisfying life.

Remember, if you feel you need help, it is an act of love and caring, and a sign of strength to seek appropriate assistance for yourself and your children. The children's drawings in Chapter 7 poignantly reveal how deeply some of them experience parental conflict, and how much they need to be helped. It does no good to blame yourself for past mistakes, you now have it in your power to correct what was wrong and to make a good life for yourself and for your children.

When you do this, you may rediscover the world through the eyes of a child, and you will likely be touched inside. Allow yourself to experience this. As you watch your child blossom you will know it was well worth it. Think about how good you will feel if your child is able to look back some day and say, "I had a good childhood. My parents both loved me very much." That would be the best launching pad you could ever give your child for his or her flight through life. The chain of unhappiness will be broken, and your life will be happier, too, as a result. So be strong, and be of good courage: your children are counting on you.

2

The Power of Mediation: Michael, and Other Case Histories

During my years of counseling, some parents who have come to me have been open to help, others have rejected it. Some have been so filled with pain and bitterness they have been unable to go beyond their own problems, others have been able to work out a viable plan for their children through divorce mediation. Here is one story of difficult mediation that resulted in a successful parenting plan.

The story of Michael, a bright eleven-year-old involved in a custody dispute, is a dramatic example of the power of the mediation process. Michael was experiencing tremendous pain, in spite of the efforts his well-meaning parents made to spare him. The three moving drawings which appear on pp. 15–16 were made in my waiting room and reveal Michael's great pain and despair. Fortunately for the child and his parents, this story has a positive ending.

Jill and Andrew, Michael's parents, were divorced six years before I first saw them. As happens to too many couples, they found themselves in court, trying to "win" custody of their son Michael, and were referred for mediation. It was not until the second session that I met their active, bright son. He was five when his parents divorced, and for a few years after the divorce he lived with his mother in a midwestern state, far away from his father. Then his mother moved back to the Los

Angeles area, and for the past year he had been living with his father.

During the first session I met with Michael's parents, neither of whom was represented by an attorney. Both were well-educated and held responsible positions. Andrew had remarried, Jill had remained single. They started out being extremely cordial to each other, but as the session went on they became more and more tense and frustrated. Each was adamant about having Michael on school days and school nights, and each proposed that Michael spend weekends and part of his vacation periods with the other parent. There was no willingness on either side to compromise. Many alternatives were discussed at length, including various joint-custody arrangements, but it soon became clear that we were at an impasse. The only thing both were able to agree upon was that Michael was under tremendous stress. Andrew said he had become very concerned about him and was taking him to a child psychiatrist. I suggested a session in which I could interview Michael. They agreed to bring him the following week.

When I interviewed Michael alone, it became apparent to me that he was in deep pain over the custody dispute. I asked, "What do you think is going on between your parents?" Michael answered, "First of all they don't talk to each other. They just argue over the phone. My mom says, 'Michael told me he wants to live with me.' Then my dad says, 'That's not what he told me. He told me he wants to live with me.' "

Michael explained that he wasn't telling them anything, "I was just listening to them."

I asked Michael how that made him feel and he replied, "Confused. It hurts me when I hear them yelling."

At my request he briefly demonstrated how his mother and father argued and then said, "It's horrible. I don't know what to do."

I asked Michael if he ever told his parents how upset he felt about their arguments and he said that he had. Then he added, "I want time to myself. This really gets to me."

When I asked him how long this arguing has been going on, he replied sadly, "For five years."

I asked Michael how he liked living with his dad and his stepmother. He answered, "Fine. I'm getting good grades."

He told me he got to see his mother every other weekend and some evenings, "but that isn't enough time." So I asked him, "Do you have some idea of how you could see your mother more often?" He responded with the following plan: "I could be with one of them on weekdays and one weekend a month, and with the other one all the other weekends and for two months in the summer."

When I asked him what he thought would happen, he answered, "The way it's going now, it's going to get worse if they don't get help."

In response to my question, "What would you like to see happen now?" Michael answered, "I wouldn't want them to get back together, that wouldn't please me. But I don't want them to fight with each other, and I don't want my mother to give me any more messages or notes for my father."

I asked Michael if he would give me permission to share what we talked about with his parents and without any hesitation he said, "Yes."

Michael's parents and stepmother then joined us in the room. In Michael's presence I summarized his interview while his parents and stepmother listened attentively. Afterward, I commented to Michael, "We all understand how upsetting this has been for you. I hope I can help your parents reach an agreement so things can be settled for you. If they can't reach an agreement here, then the judge will have to decide."

After the family conference I told Michael that I wanted to speak to his parents alone. I offered him some crayons and paper to draw on. He accepted them and walked down the hall to the waiting room.

I had hoped that what Michael had said would make a difference and help his parents settle their dispute, but they started immediately to express their deep mistrust of each other. Jill said she resented Andrew's demands. Andrew said he felt unheard. He stated his position sternly, "I want Michael to have one home." Jill cried and said, "No matter what I do he manipulates. He'd like to see me out of the picture."

I suggested that they consider sharing time more or less equally. It was then that Michael knocked on the door and brought in his drawings to show us. The three drawings clearly revealed the pain and pressure he was experiencing.

In one drawing, across the top of his paper he had drawn two heads facing each other. He had labeled one head "Mom" and the other "Dad." Out of mom's and dad's mouths in a balloon he had written, "Grrrr." Below these heads was a small boy which he had labeled "me." Out of the boy's mouth in a balloon were the words "Why oh why oh why!"

In another drawing was a boy in the middle of the paper being pulled in different directions by two hands. One hand was labeled "Mom" and the other was labeled "Dad." Each of the boy's eyes looked at a different parent. The words "No more" were coming out of both sides of the boy's mouth,

directed at each parent. Michael told me that the boy in the drawing was him and that the red streaks coming out of his chest were blood from his heart; his hands were also dripping blood. In yet another dynamic picture, he had drawn a large figure of Annie, a character from a Broadway musical and movie. She was singing, "The sun'll come out, tomorrow!" Down below, a small stick figure which he labeled "me" was saying, "I like her singing but I wish the words were true."

When Michael left the room again, I expressed my concern for his well-being. I cautioned his parents about the negative consequences for Michael should their conflict continue. Obviously, the drawings had made a great impression on them, and after some discussion they agreed to return for a third session.

Two weeks later, Jill and Andrew sat in my office again. Jill said she would agree to joint custody if Andrew would. She wanted the summers split in half. Andrew said he would be willing to expand her time with Michael to two months in the summer and overnight on Wednesday nights, in addition to alternate weekends.

After much discussion they came to a temporary agreement giving Michael equal time with each parent. They agreed to return in three months to re-evaluate this plan and to discuss a permanent parenting plan. In the meantime, Andrew said, he wanted to discuss Michael's situation with his son's psychiatrist. I suggested that Jill be included in those discussions. Both parents agreed to participate.

When Jill and Andrew returned three months later, both parents were in agreement about sharing legal and physical custody. They had attended two conferences with the psychiatrist and one with Michael's teacher. Both parents said they wanted to settle things as soon as possible to alleviate stress for Michael, and they did. They were able to work out a parenting plan that allowed Michael to spend two weekdays with Jill, three weekdays with Andrew, and alternate weekends with each parent. Since both parents lived close to Michael's school, they agreed to use the school as a buffer between homes. That way

Michael might experience less tension than if he went directly from one home to another.

The agreement was written up and signed by both parents. Before they left, I asked each of them what it was that had enabled them to reach the agreement. Jill said, "I feel less threatened now. It helped me to be able to try out a shared parenting arrangement. I see it can work. I also think Andrew and Marie feel a little more trust in me now." Andrew remarked, "I feel less threatened. I think Jill understands that I have my own life. I was concerned that she would try to interfere." Jill and Andrew agreed to return to conciliation court to re-evaluate their parenting plan before the next school year began.

Child custody mediation gave Michael's parents, stepmother, and Michael the opportunity to communicate their feelings, concerns, and needs. It also helped Michael's parents focus more on Michael's needs and on the present and future instead of on the past. The temporary agreement helped them build trust as parents and begin to develop a cooperative parenting relationship.

Without mediation Michael's parents could have gone on torturing their son for many years. Instead, they reached a good understanding and now, in time, Michael may come to believe little Annie's words, that "the sun'll come out tomorrow" after all.

Avoid Recycling Pain and Blame from the Past

Past resentments related to the marriage, such as who caused the separation and divorce, who left the other and why, painful feelings such as hurt and anger regarding the other man or other woman in the picture, disappointment, helplessness, or the desire to reconcile are all left over from the marriage.

These have nothing to do with the children and should be dealt with separately.

Nora was a distraught young mother with two girls, seven and nine years old. She told me, "I will never let them see their father." Crying, she went on to say that their father had left her and the children for another woman, that he was not to be trusted, and that she had told her girls "the truth" about their father.

I told Nora that what she was doing was harming her daughters and making them mistrust men. I explained that this would cause her daughters terrible problems later on. She answered me bitterly, "Good. I want them to mistrust men, so they won't get hurt the way I have."

When parents mix past marriage issues with present parenting issues they cause problems for their children and get little satisfaction themselves. For your child's sake, in your dealings with the other parent stick to the issues concerning your child, such as what your child needs, who will supply those needs, your concerns about your child, special problems, parents' and children's schedules, medical appointments, classes, recreational activities, and future plans.

The four-step process outlined below can assist parents in shifting gears and leaving past resentments behind:

1. Seek out and acknowledge your role, the part *you* played in creating at least some of the problems you have had, or are having, with the other parent.

2. Accept responsibility for what you did without blaming yourself or the other parent.

3. Formulate a plan for correcting and improving the situation through changes in your own attitudes and behavior.

4. Carry out your plan patiently, avoiding falling back into old patterns.

Once parents are able to accept the fact that they share responsibility, then there is no longer a need to blame each other and real headway can be made toward establishing a workable parental relationship. This is exactly what children need in order to feel loved and secure.

Minimizing the Pain for Children

Ted, a young father of a four-year-old boy, was seeing his son every other weekend. He told me with tears in his eyes, "I think it would be best if I stopped seeing Adam. He cries when I take him back to his mother's. He clings to me and won't let me go. It breaks me up. I can't stand it."

I explained to Ted that it is natural for children not to want to leave a parent, especially when they don't get to see that parent very often. I suggested that, painful as it was for him to see Adam, that he should try to see him more often and reassure him that he will be seeing him soon again. I told Ted that "gradually most children get used to the separations and can deal with them better. It takes time. Ted, if you really want to break Adam's heart, stop seeing him. He'll never get over that one."

Many parents who become estranged from their children are literally squeezed out by a short-sighted, hostile and bitter other parent who wants to get even, or who is threatened and unwilling to share. These parents can't help the way they feel, but they can help what they do. When they allow their emotions to rule them, they shortchange their children for life.

Prolonged parental conflict seriously undermines children's security and trust in their parents, in themselves, and in their own futures. Their deep mistrust, in turn, keeps them from experiencing happiness and satisfaction in their own lives—as children and when they grow up.

It is essential that parents get off to a good start following a separation, or at least very soon thereafter. Parents should make every effort to correct a bad situation. If they don't, they will find themselves stuck in a terrible nightmare, one that causes endless misery for themselves and their children. In my work, I try very hard to help parents avoid these heartaches.

Anna and Alec have a three-year-old daughter, Trina. Alec left after a fight with Anna at the suggestion of the police, who were called in by a neighbor. The next day he engaged an attorney, filed for divorce, and asked for rights to see his daughter. They came to see me just three weeks after their separation.

Anna began talking first. She said tearfully, "He's no kind of a father. He didn't even call all these days to ask about Trina. He didn't even try to see her. He doesn't love her. He wouldn't have left us if he did. Now he wants to see Trina. He drinks. I'm afraid he'll hurt her or take her away. He can only see her around me or someone in my family."

I asked Anna if Alec has been abusive to Trina in the past and if he had made any threats to take Trina away. Anna said he had not.

Next Alec spoke, "She says I don't love Trina. I was afraid to call or come to see her. I was afraid she'd call the police on me."

Anna interrupted, "Why did you change? You treated me so mean. What did I do to you?"

"I don't want to talk about it," was Alec's reply. Then he looked at me, "I'm here to talk about Trina. I want to see her twice a week, on Saturday or Sunday and on Wednesdays."

Anna refused to consider his proposal. She insisted that Alec was a danger to Trina and that his time with her must be monitored.

Alec was willing to agree to refrain from drinking, but he was totally opposed to her proposal that his visits be monitored. He stated angrily, "I've never done anything to harm Trina, even Anna said that. I've never made threats. I wouldn't take Trina away from her mother."

These parents left my office without an agreement. They were headed for court and for a decision by a judge.

I felt sad for Trina and for her parents. I knew they were

heading down a long, hard road, and wished I could have helped them avoid a battle that may never end.

Mediation is a powerful process. It is an alternative that is humane, highly effective, and appropriate for most child custody or visitation disputes. It pays for parents to give divorce mediation a try when they are unable to settle their problems and differences between themselves. The courtroom process should be resorted to only when all else fails.

3

Creating a "Conflict-Free" Zone for Your Child

If children are to succeed after divorce, they must be protected from parental conflict and allowed to enjoy close relationships with both parents. Despite pain, resentment and disagreements between them, *it is possible* for divorced parents to surround their children with a "conflict-free" zone.

The diagram on page 24 shows a child in a circle. Inside this tiny circle lies the conflict-free zone. It is surrounded by a larger circle. The space between the two circles represents a buffer zone between the child and parental conflict. The buffer zone serves as a neutral area. Parents must have the consideration and restraint to refrain from arguing or fighting when their child is present. They should save discussion of volatile issues for another time, when their child is not around. In the conflict-free zone their child is shielded from the put-downs, arguments, threats, and tension that accompany disagreements of all sorts.

This means parents must learn to control and restrain themselves in order to protect their children. It is only too easy for one embittered ex-partner to glare at the other or to make a sarcastic or snide remark. One thing leads to another, and before either side knows it the children are witnessing another argument. And they never witness it as detached spectators or observers. Because most children are attached to *both* parents, each unkind remark is like a blow felt by them. Aside from frightening them and making them miserable, imagine what this teaches them about life and about relationships. The images of this conflict will remain with them forever.

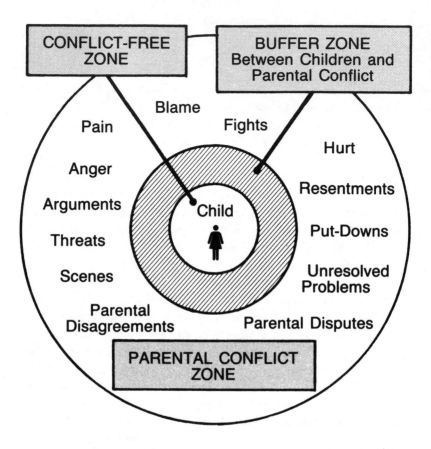

It is hard enough to raise a child right under the best of circumstances, when both parents are living together and are doing well with each other. It is much more difficult to raise a child when the parents are separated and having difficulty getting along with each other. It takes special thought, effort, and courage for divorcing parents to provide their children with a safe environment that enables them to grow up feeling good about their lives and good about themselves.

It is natural to want to blame the other parent for everything that has gone wrong and to feel like a victim; real honesty and courage are required to realize that *we* are each responsible for what happens to us. To begin with, the choice to enter into the relationship was ours. And the course of the relationship was also determined by what we did. Had we done things differently, the relationship and outcome might have been different. Once we can truly accept that we too were part of what caused the breakdown, we feel more in charge of our lives and less like victims.

Taking full responsibility for what happens to us is very difficult—but essential. Even in cases where one spouse seems to have abused the other, there are still two people making the relationship what it is. The wife who allows her husband to dominate her is as responsible as he is. If one spouse physically or verbally abuses the other, and the "abused" spouse accepts that kind of behavior, that spouse is choosing to be in that situation. The abuse would not be possible if the one who is abused would not allow it to continue.

No one wants to be treated badly, but people do tend to seek and find a relationship that suits their needs. Much of how we are treated by others depends on how we feel about ourselves. If we feel worthy of respect and love, we are more likely to choose a positive and loving situation for ourselves; if we choose otherwise, we are responsible. We learn and grow when we stop blaming others and begin to observe and change our own behavior and attitudes.

A Code of Conduct for Parent Partners

Below are some guidelines and suggestions that may help you. They represent a code of conduct, a positive guide on how to treat the other parent. If these suggestions are followed, your child will be much less likely to be caught in the crossfire of continual parental conflict. Remember, when you treat the other parent with respect, you are doing it for your child and for yourself, *not* for the other parent.

Each suggestion touches on a different aspect of the parental relationship, and each is important. The first suggestion, if followed, lays the groundwork for establishing a parental relationship after separation or divorce. The second and sixth suggestions are about the need to respect the other parent's rights to privacy and private time with the child. The third, fourth, and fifth call on parents to avoid critical and hostile interactions that escalate into conflicts. The last four suggestions encourage trust and cooperation and assist in developing positive problem-solving skills.

1. Shift gears from being marriage partners into being "parent partners."

During a marriage, parents are "husband-wife" as well as "mother-father." The diagram on page 27 shows that after a divorce they remain only "mother-father," or "parent partners."

Making the change from a husband-wife relationship to a mother-father relationship may be difficult. It requires focusing on the present and on your child's present needs, not on the past, and on your resentments and regrets. The first step is to stop blaming the other parent, and to begin to examine and acknowledge your share of the responsibility for the breakdown of the marriage.

2. Settle disagreements through give-and-take and compromise, and respect individual differences.

It is difficult to give in, especially when you feel hurt, threatened, or controlled. So when the other parent asks you for a favor or change of schedule it may seem satisfying to say no. Chances are that the next time you want something changed or rearranged, you will also get no for an answer. Small disagreements then escalate into bigger ones, and in this struggle the one who gets hurt is your child.

I strongly recommend that you say yes to the other parent whenever you can, and compromise whenever possible. This does not mean you should allow yourself to be taken advantage of, it means you should be flexible.

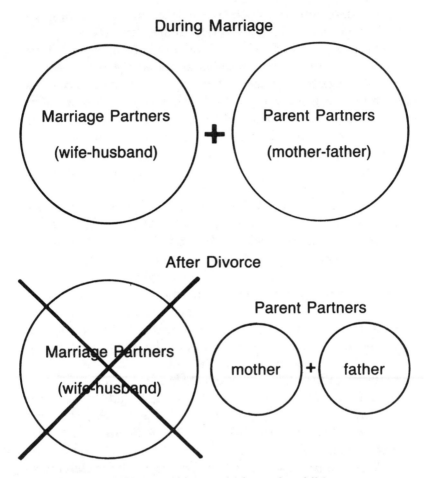

During Marriage

Marriage Partners (wife-husband) **+** Parent Partners (mother-father)

After Divorce

Marriage Partners (wife-husband)

Parent Partners

mother **+** father

Ron asked Sharon if he could keep the children one extra day to attend a special family gathering. Sharon said, "No, it's not your day!" She clicked the receiver down hard in Ron's ear.

People usually find a way to get even, and Ron did. When Sharon asked Ron to change the schedule so she could take the children to her company picnic, Ron refused.

Ron and Sharon's struggle caused the children to miss *two* important occasions and caused many hard feelings between the parents. It would have been far better for them to have given a little extra consideration to each other, thus heading off frustration and pain for their children and themselves.

In order to avoid constant hassles and arguments, it is essential that parents learn to avoid power struggles and respect the differences between them. There are hundreds of issues that parents can argue and fight about. They can argue over differences in life-style, religious beliefs, values, the children's proper bedtime, what foods the children should eat, how often they should be bathed, what recreation and sports they should be offered, whether or not the children's teeth need to be straightened, which doctor to use, and so on. The list is endless.

Two parents I counseled were in a dispute over the children's religious education. Linda believed that their children should attend Sunday school, but Ed did not believe in organized religion. Ed said he refused to be "a phony" by telling the children he believed in their religion when he didn't, despite Linda's expectation that he do so.

I explained to Linda and Ed that it is not uncommon for two parents—even husbands and wives—to feel differently on a number of issues, including religion. That is the way life is. Each parent has a unique point of view and the right to share it with his or her children. When there are differences of opinion, parents should tell their children, "Daddy and I (or Mommy and I) see things differently." Then each parent can tell them what he or she believes without belittling the other parent's point of view.

In this case, Linda had the right to send her children to Sunday school if she wanted when the children were with her, and Ed could choose not to send them.

When parents continually argue, their children get caught in the middle. They worry constantly about having to take sides or pleasing both parents. Children should understand that it is natural and all right for people to have differing points of view. As they grow up, they will see things their own way anyway. It is important for parents not to try to sway children to accept their way of thinking and to teach respect for individual differences.

3. Treat the other parent with respect, and avoid making derogatory statements about the other parent in the presence of your child.

You don't have to like the other parent to say hello when he or she calls on the telephone or comes to pick up the child. You would probably show a total stranger that much respect. When you treat the other parent in a civil, cordial manner, it helps create a more harmonious environment for you and your child.

Children need to look up to both parents. When one parent treats the other badly or makes derogatory remarks to the children about him or her, children are caught in the middle and forced to take sides. This in turn causes them to feel extremely uncomfortable and pressured, which is not at all what they need in order to feel good about themselves and to succeed.

Not long ago I interviewed a ten-year-old boy alone. When I asked him how he was getting along with his father, he hesitated.

I asked, "Is there some problem you're having with your dad?"

He replied, "My dad always says bad things about my mom. He says she isn't a good mom. The things he says about her are not true."

I asked, "How does that make you feel about your dad?"

He answered angrily, "I don't like it. I ask him to stop but he keeps on doing it."

4. Avoid arguments, scenes, threats, fights, and violence, especially when your child is present.

Children tell me how frightened and helpless they feel when their parents argue or fight. No matter how upset the adults are, how angry they may feel, and how much they feel like hurting the other parent for causing them pain, for their children's sake they *must* avoid threats, violence, and confrontations in front of their children.

Twelve-year-old Marc told me sadly, "My dad came over and ruined my birthday. He called my mom names and accused her of untrue things. My dad drinks a lot. I wish he'd stop drinking and get help for himself. I'm really mad at him."

Threats and violence can lead to terrible problems for children and parents alike. Ron, a young father of a two-year-old son, found it hard even to talk to me about what happened. He sat for a while with his head in his hands. Then he began to speak, "It was terrible. Sue forced me to leave the house. I was having so many pressures. Sue was going out on me. I pleaded with her to take me back but she wouldn't." The next day Ron pushed his way into the house against Sue's wishes and refused to leave. He grabbed her and shook her to try to make her understand his feelings. A neighbor called the police, who came and escorted Ron out. Ron went home and telephoned Sue. "I told her I was coming to kill her. I really didn't mean it," he told me. This time the police arrested Ron on the basis of a complaint made by Sue.

While Ron waited outside my office, Sue told me her side of it. There had been previous incidents of violence, and she had gone to court to get a restraining order to force Ron to leave the house. When he pushed his way in and refused to leave, she tried to get out but he wouldn't let her go. He grabbed her and she screamed. A neighbor called the police. Their son watched the whole incident. Sue said tearfully, "Later that day Ron threatened to kill both me and our son. I'm afraid to let our son go with Ron alone unless he gets some help for himself."

Because of the threats and violence, Sue had initiated a case to limit Ron's visitation rights. By the time I saw them Sue wasn't willing to settle things. She wanted the judge to order monitored visitation for Ron, so he could visit his son only in the presence of a third party. Ron wasn't willing to agree to that. So the battle continues.

The ones who suffer most in this kind of case are the children. Sometimes, as a result of threats or violence, the frightened parent will move far away, and the children lose a parent in the process. Parents who are genuinely concerned about their children's well-being will avoid confrontations in front of the children. They can discuss sensitive issues over the telephone or at private meetings out of the presence of their children, or by mail. Child support payments should be sent ahead, and not given when picking up or returning the children.

The wish of almost every child I interview is that their parents not argue or fight. Only parents can grant this wish. I suggest they experience their own hurt and anger without acting them out, and especially not in front of their children. Parents who can't control their anger owe it to themselves and their offspring to seek help.

5. Don't be overly critical or try to control the other parent.

Unless your child is really at risk or in danger while with the other parent, it is advisable not to be picky, critical, or too demanding. Let small concerns or irritations pass. For instance, if the other parent is a few minutes late once in a while, it is better not to make a fuss about it. Instead, discuss major issues that concern your rights, or your child's health, safety, education, and welfare.

The way you tell the other parent about your concerns will make a difference in the way that parent responds to you. If you demand, attack, blame, or threaten, you will get a defensive response. Threatening statements, such as, "If you ever take my children around to your girlfriend's (or boyfriend's), I'll never let you take them again," or, "If you come even five minutes late, I'll be gone and you'll just have to miss seeing the children this week," will only anger the other person—and provoke them to retaliate.

Even when you feel annoyed and furious with the other parent, keep the peace for your child's sake. State your complaints in a positive manner without being abusive, sarcastic, or overly demanding. If, for example, you are upset or inconvenienced by some behavior of the other parent, or if there is something special you wish to ask or communicate to him or her, say what it is that you wish or need or are concerned about without being defensive or bringing up the past. If you can't control yourself in person, then write a cordial note.

Some positive examples are: "I begin to worry when you are more than a half-hour late returning Johnny. Please give me a call if you're running late. I would really appreciate this." Or, "Please put in an extra change of clothes and a warm jacket this week. We're planning to go camping, and I want to be sure Dana stays dry and warm." Or, "Please remember to give Lisa her medicine. Dr. Henry said she should have it four times a day. The directions are on the bottle. Thanks."

6. Avoid pressuring the other parent about getting back together again, and respect the other parent's privacy.

Trying to persuade the other parent to reconcile when he or she does not want to will not only cause problems for your child but also increase your feelings of frustration and rejection. If your former husband or wife wanted to be with you again, he or she would find a way for you to be together.

After their separation, Ned telephoned Dianne at work almost every day, and sometimes several times a day, to talk to her about getting back together. This was after Dianne had made it very clear to Ned that the marriage was over. He was very persistent and would become so upset when she wasn't seeing things his way that he would become abusive. He had hit Dianne a number of times in the past, and now threatened that if Dianne were ever to bring another man near his son, he couldn't say what he might do. Ned also insisted on discussing the possibility of reconciliation every time he came to pick up Andrew, their four-year-old son. There had been frequent arguments and even a few violent scenes in front of the child.

Dianne felt she had to do something to protect herself and Andrew from Ned's tirades and violence, so she moved two thousand miles away. Ned lost not only Dianne but his son as well. Now he sees Andrew for only a few weeks each year, a situation that he helped to create, and a tremendous loss for both father and son.

Ned couldn't be blamed for feeling lost and devastated over the end of his marriage; that was understandable. But he could help what he said to Dianne and the way he behaved toward her. She had a right to her own life and her privacy. Ned could *not* force her to stay with him, and he had no right to keep harassing her, especially to threaten to harm her in any way.

Ned would have been far better off if he had sought the services of a professional counselor, psychologist, or psychiatrist for support and help in getting through this difficult time.

7. Don't sacrifice your child over money.

There are some parents who refuse to agree to anything until all financial issues are settled. Financial settlements can take years. In the meantime, children should not be kept hanging in the balance. As soon as the separation occurs, parents should cooperate in making suitable and appropriate arrangements for their children so that they can have time with both parents.

No matter how upset and frustrated parents may be over unresolved financial issues, they should respect their child's right to see both parents under a workable, peaceable arrangement.

Disputes over which parent will keep the house can be agonizing for some children. Sharon and Ian continued to live in the same home because neither was willing to leave. This led to constant arguments and quarrels, which their two children witnessed daily. Also, they fought over who would have the children each day. It was almost two years before the financial situation was settled. In the meantime the children were tormented by their parents' lack of sensitivity, respect, and cooperation. Their six-year-old daughter Amy told me, "Some days I can't say hello to my daddy, because my mommy says it is not his day. When it's my daddy's day, I can't say hello to my mommy."

The situation was even worse for Carl and Jane's two teenage children. The parents were so busy quarreling over the financial issues that neither of them was willing to make a home for their children until everything was settled. Jane was living with her mother. She said, "There's no room for the children there. When I get some money, I'll get my own place and take the children." Carl lived in a bachelor apartment where they didn't allow children. He said, "If Jane will agree to the financial settlement, I'll get a bigger apartment and take the children."

Both parents were working. Each blamed the other for delays in settling the financial situation and each wanted the other to take responsibility for their children.

Jane put their thirteen-year-old son Gary and all his belongings outside her door one day and called Carl to come and pick him up. Carl came to get him, but since no children were allowed to live in his building, Gary had to sneak in the back way. His parents told me that Gary threatened suicide several times during the next few months.

Jane sent their daughter Carla away to a boarding school, and Carla couldn't come home on weekends because both her parents demanded that the other parent keep her. With summer vacation coming, Carla was faced with having nowhere to go unless her parents' finances were settled. Long after such situations occur, scars will remain.

8. Pay child support payments on time.

This will help avoid arguments between you and the other parent. It will also help keep your child's life running smoothly. Child support is an important parental responsibility. The purpose is to try to equalize the quality of life for children in both homes.

Children should not be burdened with support problems or be made to ask for it. When parents cannot come to an agreement about child support, they should let the court decide the issue. Once a decision has been made, child support payments should be paid regularly and promptly. If a parent refuses to pay, the other parent can call on the district attorney's office for assistance.

As important as child support payments are, children should *not* be kept from seeing a parent because the payment has not been made. Money issues and parent-child relationship issues are separate and should be kept separate. If they are not, children not only lose financial support but also valuable and needed time with a parent. This is a double punishment for your child.

One small boy told me, "I can't see my daddy because he doesn't pay child support. If he loved me he would pay."

If this child is not helped to feel loved and he grows up with low self-esteem, he will have little chance of being happy and successful. His father will be partly responsible because he did not send child support payments in on time and his mother will be partly responsible for his misfortune by mixing money issues with visitation issues. Unfortunately, their son will be the one who will pay the price for their uncooperative behavior.

9. Gain the other parent's trust as a parent by keeping any agreements and promises you make.

Rebuilding trust between divorced parents is essential. It helps them create the conflict-free zone in which their children can thrive. When agreements are not kept, anger, disappointment, hostility, resentment, grudges, and retaliation follow. Before long the situation becomes terrible for the children involved, as in the cases described below.

After Bob returned the children to Leslie hours late on Mother's Day, Leslie retaliated by refusing to give Bob the children at all on Father's Day. They were in court two months later.

When Fran was not home at the agreed-upon time to receive the children, Roy waited around for half an hour or so, then left with the children. Later that evening a big argument ensued over the telephone. Their children overheard and trembled.

A mother of a two-year-old told me, "I can't trust Mike. He gets busy doing stuff and he doesn't watch Scott. Scott got hurt twice when he was at his dad's place. Mike leaves his tools around and Scott could hurt himself real bad on his saws. He also doesn't always use the car seat."

A father of a nine-year-old told me worriedly, "Lisa left my son asleep and went to the store. What if a fire had broken out?"

The best way to build trust is by being a responsible parent. This means caring for your child in a safe and responsible way without giving the other parent anything to complain or worry about in this regard. Babies and young children need to have the constant supervision and protection of an adult. Older children and adolescents also need parental supervision appropriate to their age.

10. Accept the fact that each parent has the right to spend time with his or her child, and the child has the right to a relationship with each parent.

If you can accept this, it will relieve the child of a great burden, and the child will then be free to have a relationship with the other parent. Many children suffer greatly when deprived by divorce of the presence of one parent. If they also lose their relationship with that parent, they will be made even more miserable, because they are not being allowed to recover and heal after the divorce.

Janet and Paul had been divorced seven years. Their children, Karen, age fifteen, and Eric, age eleven, lived with Janet and saw Paul whenever Janet would let them.

Paul wanted custody of both his children. Eric wanted to live with him. He told me, "Janet grounds my kids and won't let them see me or talk to me on the phone. I have always supported them, but she has turned my kids against me."

Janet wanted to continue to have custody. "I believe in disciplining my kids," she said. "I took away their privilege to see their father as a punishment for a few months. Then a counselor I saw told me I couldn't do that. She said I should take other privileges away from them. They didn't complain about not seeing their father. They weren't anxious to go. My whole life is those kids." Tears came to her eyes as she spoke.

Janet continued, "My main concern is for Paul to stop badgering the kids to live with him and stop talking against me to the kids." Paul acknowledged that during the last few months he had been trying to persuade the children to live with him, but he had made a vow not to do it anymore.

I talked to their daughter, Karen, and asked her if she remembered when her parents had separated. She replied, "I remember my dad packing and leaving, and him visiting. I remember crying and telling him not to go, but you get over it."

Karen told me that she had been seeing her father about once a month, which was often enough because of her many activities. How did she feel about being pressured to live with her father, I asked. She said, "You don't know what to say after he asks that. A couple of times I said yes, but most of the time I didn't say anything. It made me feel uncomfortable. I wish everything would calm down and settle out."

Their son, Eric, told me, "My parents are always fighting and aggravating. My mom aggravates my dad. When we are grounded we can't see my dad, but we can go to the movies. That's not fair to my dad. I want to live with my dad. I really want to."

"Did you tell your mother?" I asked.

Eric replied, "I told her and she said, 'I don't ever want to see you again.' Later she told my dad to send me home. I want to live with my dad and see my mom some weekends."

Eric's indignation toward his mother and his resentment of her refusal to respect his father's right to see him is a fairly common occurrence. Once children are old enough and wise enough to understand and protest against unfair parental attitudes and practices, they rebel. Many of these children want to leave the "unfair" parent to live with the other.

For such children the loss is tremendous, and the continuing conflicts prolong the agony. Moreover, when people are made unhappy or miserable as children they tend to re-enact their unresolved conflicts in adulthood. None of this sadness and tragedy need happen, if parents are willing to work cooperatively with one another.

Cooperate in Raising the Children

Helping your child succeed after divorce requires cooperation between you and the other parent. Cooperation means:

— Settling on a workable parenting plan that gives children access to both parents

— Keeping ongoing contact with the children so they don't feel rejected or abandoned

— Preparing the children beforehand for the separation, if possible

— Reassuring children that they can still count on both parents

— Taking the parenting plan seriously

— Never disappointing children at the last minute

— Rarely canceling plans with children

— Each parent establishing a home for the children with a place for their clothes, toys, and other possessions

— Maintaining telephone contact with the children

— Providing children telephone access to both parents

— Having children ready on time for the other parent

— Being home to receive the children on time

— Calling the other parent when it is necessary to be late

— Setting up a "hot line" between parents for discussion of serious problems concerning the children

Cooperation creates the kind of environment in which children feel safe, satisfied, and loved. Cooperation does *not* mean:

— Pumping children for information about the other parent

— Trying to control the other parent

— Using the children to carry angry messages back and forth

— Using children to deliver child support payments

— Arguing in front of the children

— Speaking derogatorily about the other parent

— Asking the children with whom they want to live

— Putting the children in the position of having to take sides

There are many advantages for parents who choose to cooperate and work together on raising their children after divorce. Here are a few:

— Fewer problems for the children

— More personal satisfaction and less frustration for the parents

— Fewer visitation problems

— Fewer child support problems

— Less going back to court

— Easier sharing of responsibility

— Better parent-child relationships

— More freedom from conflict

— Fewer health, emotional, school, and social problems

A Thought for the Future

During the chaotic and emotional period of separation and divorce parents may think it impossible to get along or cooperate with each other. It is a period of great pain, involving feelings of guilt and failure, the loss of security, friendship and love, and having to deal with some less-attractive aspects of oneself such as revenge, bitterness, and great anger. It is a trial by fire, and for many, the hardest time of their lives. Individually and as a society we need to find ways to encourage and help divorcing parents think of the future—their child's and their own. One parent said to me that looking back, she felt that what had actually freed her from the vicious cycle of guilt, pain and anger that overwhelmed her after the divorce was being forced to go outside herself, having to put the needs of her children before her own. In the longer term, the ability to deal with her her ex-spouse in a controlled way *because she was thinking of someone else* gradually restored her self-esteem and allowed her to heal herself.

4

Joint Custody: Sparing Your Child by Sharing Your Child

For some parents, having to share parenthood with the former partner is a sensitive and painful thing to do. Yet sharing a child is one of the best ways parents can show their love and caring for their child. A possessive attitude often stems from one parent feeling threatened that he or she will be controlled by the other parent or will lose the child. For many parents the very thought of sharing the children with a former spouse is frightening. They can't imagine how they can possibly get along with a former partner after a divorce when they couldn't get along during the marriage. In her book *Mom's House / Dad's House*, Dr. Isolina Ricci points out that parents do not *have* to like the other parent or be friends in order to work together cooperatively regarding their children. They can learn to develop a "working relationship," which is similar to the relationship between business partners.

There is a wide variety of parenting plans from which to choose, ranging all the way from one parent having sole or primary custody and most of the responsibility for raising the child to both parents having joint custody and sharing the responsibility more or less equally.

A suitable parenting plan or arrangement should have the children's best interests and needs in mind, as well as the parents' needs, preferences, and schedules. The following factors should be considered: (1) the plan should allow both parents to allow both parents to have significant amounts of time with their child; (2) school-age children and adolescents should be able to attend school and take part in activities regularly; (3) infants and younger children should see and spend time with both parents frequently; (4) parents' work schedules must be allowed for; (5) some flexibility is needed and provision should be made for making changes; and (6) the plan should be re-evaluated periodically in terms of the children's progress and modified, if necessary, to meet the children's changing needs.

Consider Shared Parenting or Joint Custody

Some parents believe that if they get sole custody of the children, they won't ever have to deal with the other parent again. In reality they *will* have to deal with the other parent as long as they and their children are alive. Other parents believe that joint custody means that their child *must* live with one parent for six months, then with the other parent for six months, and will have to change schools every semester. This is a fundamental misunderstanding, and it is no wonder that most parents are against that idea. So am I!

There are two legal terms connected with joint custody: "joint legal custody" and "joint physical custody." Joint legal custody means that both parents have an equal say in major decisions regarding their children's health, education, and general welfare. For example, both parents have the right to go to their children's schools, speak to their children's teachers, receive progress reports, and to attend parent-teacher conferences, school open houses, and special activities at which parents are permitted. Both parents also have the right to obtain emergency medical treatment for their children at hospitals, speak with their children's doctors and dentists, obtain information and medical records, request additional medical consultations, and so on.

Joint physical custody means that each parent takes a turn

in sharing responsibility for his or her child's care. A parenting plan is worked out, which states when each parent is responsible for his or her child. A child then has two homes and lives with the mother part of the time and with the father part of the time. There are many kinds of joint custody plans from which to choose. The particular plan that parents select should make sense for each child, and adjustments should be made to meet the changing needs of the child.

Several states in the U.S.A have adopted joint custody legislation. The goals of this legislation are to ensure that minor children will have frequent and ongoing contact with both parents after they have separated or divorced, and to encourage parents to share responsibility for their children.

What do parents and children have to gain from sharing custody? I believe there are many advantages. First of all, it is natural for each parent to continue to have responsibility for raising a child after divorce. Each was a parent beforehand, and it is natural and fitting for them to continue to share that responsibility.

One serious concern for many women is a financial one. Their biggest worry about giving the children to the father half of the time is that they will not get child support. If a woman earns as much as a man does, she may not; however, if he earns substantially more than she does, he would ordinarily still be asked to contribute more than she does toward the children's support. The deciding issue here is that he has the ability to pay more than she does, and not whether he has the children half the time.

A second important advantage is that sharing custody encourages both parents to remain involved in their children's lives and to assume parental duties and responsibilities. This is an important advantage when one considers the fact that approximately one-third of the children of divorce completely lose contact with one of their parents.

A third advantage is that shared custody arrangements meet children's needs. Children tend to progress well and feel better about themselves when they have close and continuous contact with both of their parents.

Shared custody arrangements meet parental needs too. Joint custody parents have the same rights and shared responsibilities; this avoids one parent becoming completely overburdened and burned out from trying to do everything alone. In shared custody arrangements, each parent has significant amounts of time with the children and time without the children. This enables them to maintain close relationships with their children, as well as build a life and other relationships for themselves.

Shared custody equalizes the balance of power between parents, giving neither one more than the other. Psychologically speaking, parents who share custody tend to feel less threatened about losing their children than a noncustodial parent would. This balance of power is likely to generate fewer power struggles, less need to compete, less litigation, less tugging back and forth on the children, and an all-round better outcome for the children.

Some False Assumptions About Joint Custody

The main arguments raised by parents and even some professionals against joint custody are:

1. Children need the stability of one home. Going back and forth is too hard on children and too disruptive.

2. Mothers are more suited to caring for children than fathers.

3. Divorcing parents cannot get along well enough to share custody.

4. Joint custody will lead to more hassles, arguments, and litigation.

These arguments were repudiated in a research study done at the Philadelphia Child Guidance Clinic (See *References*, 1.) Of the forty-three families studied by Deborah Ann Leupnitz, Ph.D., 55 percent of the single-custody parents returned to court at least once over money or visitation issues, while none of the joint-custody parents did so in spite of disagreements. Dr. Leupnitz's study also showed that joint-custody fathers supported their children reliably, that children whose parents shared custody were pleased and comfortable with the arrangement, and that joint-custody parents did not feel as overwhelmed by the pressure of raising a child alone as the single-custody parents did. Another study done earlier, which compared litigation following sole-custody awards with joint-custody awards, showed significantly less litigation following joint-custody awards even when parents were ordered to have joint custody against their will (See *References*, 2.)

In my opinion, security for a child is based on close and loving relationships with both parents and not necessarily on being tucked into the same little bed every night. In matters of comfort and lifestyle, children are very adaptive and resilient. They can adjust to many changes and schedules as long as they are not fought over continually and not deprived of their parents. In the United States most mothers work and less than 13 percent of them stay home with their children. From an early age, the children are bundled up and taken to babysitters, where they spend most of their waking hours. Yet many of these working mothers object to having the children spend time at the father's home because it would be too disruptive. This is inconsistent and self-serving. Fathers can be nurturing parents too. Women's liberation has freed men to become more involved fathers.

I see it as a strongly positive sign that more and more fathers are asking for joint custody and more meaningful involvement in their children's lives. Children certainly need *two* involved parents. After divorce, parents *can* learn how to get along and share parenting responsibilities, even if they were not able to get along as husband and wife.

Historically, child custody has now come full circle. Until about one hundred years ago fathers usually got custody of the children, because at that time fathers were at home, working their farms. Once men began to work in factories and mothers remained at home with the children, mothers were awarded custody. Now that most mothers and fathers both work, the pendulum is beginning to swing back to center toward both parents sharing custody, and toward both parents continuing to raise the children after divorce. Within a decade I predict it will be the norm, rather than the exception.

Work Out a Suitable Parenting Plan

No matter what form of custody arrangement you desire or choose, it is critical that you and the other parent work out a suitable parenting plan as soon as possible. The following paragraphs contain some suggestions for shared physical custody plans and shared parenting plans.

When parents live fairly close to each other, they can share physical custody in a number of ways. Their children can spend alternative weekends and two days each week with each parent, or half of the week with each, or full weeks on an alternating basis. For younger children frequent access to both parents is important, since a whole week is a very long time for a young child to be without either parent. For school-age children, alternate weeks with each parent, or more time with one parent during weekdays and more weekend and vacation time with the other are appropriate plans. In planning for adolescents, schedules should be somewhat flexible to accommodate their activities.

When parents live far apart, the children can spend the school year with one parent and most of their vacation time with the other parent. This plan can be alternated every two or three years. Rotating too often might disrupt a child's education and activities.

Parents can be as creative as they like in developing a

shared parenting plan as long as the plan they select has the children's ages, needs, and schedules in mind. Children should be observed closely to see if they are doing well with the plan parents have selected. Changes in schedules may be needed as situations change and needs change. It is important that the spirit of joint custody remains, namely, that parents share rights and responsibilities and that the children have two homes, one with mom and one with dad. Parents usually share driving children to school and activities. Children have clothes, toys, and friends in both homes. In this way, neither parent is seen as a visitor by the children.

A suitable parenting arrangement can give both you and your child much-needed structure and security. It will help your child feel less confused, and less worried about losing you or losing the other parent. Once a workable parenting arrangement is agreed upon, or ordered by the court, it should be taken seriously. Only in case of real emergency or necessity should it be canceled, although changes can be made by mutual agreement between parents.

Special Considerations for Infants and Young Children

Infants and very young children need frequent access to both parents. Therefore, an arrangement that allows the infant or young child to spend time with the other parent often, such as every few days, is preferable to plans that allow the young child to see the other parent only weekly or twice a month.

When an infant or young child does not know or remember one parent, every effort should be made to help the child develop a close relationship with that parent, in order to avoid problems later on. If a parent has not had contact with an infant or young child before, or not for a period of time, the first few visits should be brief and spaced fairly close together, preferably with a mutually agreed-upon third person present who the child knows. This allows the child to get acquainted or reacquainted with that parent and is less frightening than an unexpected longer visit with a total stranger. It does require cooperation on the part of both parents, some patience, and a certain amount of inconvenience; however, it is less traumatic to do it this way for the infant or young child. As the child becomes familiar and comfortable with that parent, the length of the visits can gradually be increased to an entire day, to one overnight, to entire weekends, and so on.

Rita and Ron's eight-month-old infant was just three months old when they separated. Ron was rarely allowed to see his son and then only in Rita's presence. He told me angrily, "He's my son, too. I have as much right to him as she does. I want him every other weekend."

Rita responded, "He's too young to go. You never took care of him, you were always out drinking with your friends. You're only interested in him now because your mother wants to see him." She looked at Ron with tremendous anger.

I asked Rita, "What are you most angry at Ron for?"

She burst into tears, "Ron wants to take my baby. I'm still nursing him. Maybe when he's older. Ron doesn't know how to take care of him."

I hear this story so often from mothers of young babies. It is so hard for them to let go of their infants. In part, this has to do with the symbiotic tie that exists between an infant and mother from the time when the baby was in the womb, a bond that is both physical and psychological. This tie continues after birth and causes mother and infant to feel as one unit, bonded together. Nursing mothers and their infants are especially tied to each other. Fortunately, now that many fathers are involved in the birthing process and in caring for their young infants right from birth, they also can experience a close bonding with their infants.

Difficult as it may be for a mother of a young infant to let go of her baby, it is essential that the infant spend time with the father also. The father should be given a list of instructions by the mother regarding feeding and care of their baby. Short periods away from the mother can gradually be expanded into longer and longer periods as the child grows. During times when the mother is working or is not available to take care of her child, the father should be given first right to provide care for his child if he can do so. This helps the father and the infant to develop the close relationship that the child needs. Children are happiest and liveliest when both parents are involved in their lives, and when they feel close and comfortable with both parents, each of whom feeds and cares for them during specified periods.

Arrangements for School-age Children

School-age children benefit from longer periods with each parent, including spending some nights in the father's as well as the mother's home. Children of this age need to be encouraged to love both parents and also stepparents, grandparents, and relatives from both sides of the family. Parenting arrangements should allow school-age children to participate in social, sports, and recreational activities connected with their school. Ideally, both parents should be involved in their child's education and should encourage him or her to do homework assignments. In each home the child should be provided with a place to study and an atmosphere in which he or she can be free from commotion and television. Children should always be taken to school on time, and should not miss school except for illness, or an occasional day or two for an important reason.

Arrangements for Adolescents

Adolescents need to be allowed to pursue their own interests and social relationships. They should not be expected to stay home and hold Mom's or Dad's hand. They need freedom from overwhelming responsibility for major family decisions. They need parents who act like parents, not like pals; parents who do not constantly lean on *them* for moral support; cooperative parents who do not pressure them to take sides. Because they are not yet mature, they need ongoing contact with both parents and continued guidance about rules and standards for their behavior. At the same time, they need privacy, activities with other adolescents, and some flexibility concerning schedules. Admittedly, working around an adolescent's schedule can be frustrating for parents, but they need to make the effort.

Cindy, age fifteen, told me, "My problem is that I play in a girl's softball league and sometimes we have games or practices when I'm supposed to be with my dad. My dad gets upset. He says he only gets to see me every other weekend and it ruins his plans. He blames my mom for letting me sign up for the league. It's not her fault. I wanted to play."

It is natural for adolescents to want to be involved in activities, and it is hard for them to keep their parents happy and still satisfy themselves. There is no simple solution. Occasionally, the adolescent could compromise by missing a practice or event; at other times, parents could change their schedules to accommodate the adolescent's plans. Even though parental rights to see the child should be respected, some flexibility is essential.

Avoid Holiday Hassles

The holiday season can be an especially lonely time for single parents without their children. When there are hassles regarding holiday schedules, no one enjoys the holidays. However, with some forethought and planning you can create enjoyable holiday arrangements for yourself and your children. Since Christmas is often the most sensitive holiday, I will use it as an example.

Here are several possible ways that parents can work out the Christmas holiday:

1. Children could spend Christmas Eve through Christmas morning at 9:00 or 10:00 A.M. with one parent;

Christmas Day through December 26 at 9:00 or 10:00 A.M. with the other; then reverse this order the following year.

2. Children could spend the entire Christmas holiday with one parent one year and with the other parent the following year; thus each parent would have the children every other year.

3. Children could spend Christmas morning with one parent and Christmas afternoon with the other and reverse this the following year.

4. Children could spend Christmas Eve with one parent and Christmas Day with the other every year, if parents prefer this because of family traditions.

5. Parents could spend the holidays together with the children, if both feel comfortable doing so.

There is no end to the holiday hassles experienced by some children of divorce, and the effects can continue long after they have grown up. I counseled a couple of newlyweds who were on the verge of splitting up after an argument over Christmas arrangements. Julie had told Andrew that she didn't think it was fair that they had spent only a few hours with her parents and had spent most of the holiday seeing both of his parents, who were divorced. Andrew had exploded. He was too upset to discuss it, or be supportive to his young bride.

During our counseling session I explored this sensitive issue with Andrew. He told me that he still felt tremendous pressure to please both of his parents during the holidays, each of whom "still pressure me to spend Christmas with them." He had tried hard to work out a plan that would accommodate his parents and also his new wife and her parents, an overwhelming task. If he had discussed this problem with Julie before the holiday, or asked her to help him work it out, she might have been more sympathetic. But when she complained, he just couldn't handle it emotionally.

Andrew told Julie and me, "Every year I feel like going away by myself for Christmas, so I don't have to deal with them. That's what my sister does."

We can see that, in addition to ruining Andrew's Christmases, his parents' competitiveness about the holidays even jeopardized their son's marriage.

I encourage parents to work out a holiday plan so that the children can enjoy all of their holidays. For the times that parents do not have the children, I suggest they make plans for themselves with friends or family, so they do not have to be alone. On the following page is a sample holiday chart that can help parents plan holiday arrangements.

If No Agreement Can Be Reached, Seek Help

Parents who find they are quarreling over their children and are unable to settle on a suitable parenting plan should seek help; otherwise their conflict may escalate into a battle that could be traumatic for the children.

Adam, a sensitive ten-and-a-half-year-old boy involved in a hot custody dispute, had witnessed many physical fights between his parents. Bad memories of these fights could remain with him for life.

On page 57 is the picture Adam drew of the war that was going on between his parents. He drew his mother and father on two separate battleships, facing and firing at each other. He drew a submarine below the water, between the two battleships. He labeled the submarine "the children." He also drew a plane overhead. From the plane in a bubble Adam wrote the words, "Stop! Stop!" Beside the plane he wrote "the counselor."

In his drawing Adam appeared to be asking me to help him end the war between his parents. This was not an easy task. His parents had been fighting for years. They were each

HOLIDAY AND VACATION SCHEDULE

Holiday and vacation schedules take precedence over regular schedules.
Holidays for Mother: Every Mother's Day and Mother's birthday.
Holidays for Father: Every Father's Day and Father's birthday.

HOLIDAY	TIME	EVEN YEARS	ODD YEARS
New Year's Day		Father	Mother
Presidents' Day Weekend		Mother	Father
Easter		Father	Mother
Passover		Mother	Father
Memorial Day Weekend		Father	Mother
July 4th		Mother	Father
Labor Day Weekend		Father	Mother
Halloween		Mother	Father
Thanksgiving		Father	Mother
Chanukah		Mother	Father
Christmas Eve		Father	Mother
Christmas Day		Mother	Father
Child(ren)'s Birthday(s)		Father	Mother
Other			

VACATION SCHEDULE	EVEN YEARS	ODD YEARS
Easter Vacation — 1st Half	Mother	Father
Easter Vacation — 2nd Half	Father	Mother
Summer Vacation Schedule	Two weeks with each parent, to be arranged by agreement, plus additional time for the parent having less time with the children during the school year.	
Christmas Vacation — 1st Half	Father	Mother
Christmas Vacation — 2nd Half	Mother	Father

deeply entrenched in their own positions and Adam was hope-
lessly caught in the middle. Across the top of his drawing in
large letters Adam wrote with black crayon:

"THE PROBLEMES WITH DIVORCES
IS THEY TURN INTO WOARS."

Susan and John were referred to me for mediation when
they were in court litigating over visitation issues regarding
Adam. John had remarried, Susan had not. They also had a
nineteen-year-old daughter who had lived with her boyfriend
since the separation and was not involved in the court proceedings. Fortunately for Adam, his parents were finally able to
reach an amicable agreement after several sessions of child
custody mediation. As such, they are to be congratulated. Difficult as it was for them to meet and to communicate, they per-
sisted until a parenting agreement was reached. They did this
out of love for their son. Their struggles and their triumphs are
described below.

Adam's parents had been separated two years. During that
time, Adam had been living with his mother and seeing his father irregularly, according to his father, and regularly, according
to his mother. The parents lived approximately an hour's driving time apart.

At the first meeting, Susan and John sat tensely in my office as I explained the purpose of the mediation session. If they
were able to reach an agreement about Adam, I told them, I
could write it up for them and this would make it unnecessary
for the judge to make the decision.

I gave them the choice of who would go first to tell me his
or her perceptions of the situation and to give me an idea of
what each wanted to see happen.

John spoke first, grimly, "I have joint custody but the
problem is maintaining contact with my son. I am supposed
to have reasonable visitation rights, but Susan will only per-
mit me to see Adam three nights a month. She punishes me
and uses Adam as a weapon. This weekend, for example, she
refused to let Adam go with me, after I understood I could pick
him up. She refuses to help with the driving at all.

"I want more time with Adam, at least what is standard for the courts to allow. I want half of the summer and I want a definite plan so I don't have to beg her for time to see my son."

John proposed the following schedule: on alternate weeks from Friday after school until Wednesday at 8:30 A.M. and on the other weeks either Monday or Tuesday evening overnight; on alternate holidays; one-half of Christmas vacation; one-half of Easter vacation; on Father's Day and on his own birthday.

Susan said, "It was very difficult when he left us. I tried hard to do everything for Adam. I took him to a counselor. I even let John use my house but he abused my privacy. He used my phone and drank my wine."

She continued, "Adam is confused. He is insecure. John took him to San Francisco for his wedding and made Adam fly back on a plane alone. I offered him half of last weekend, but he came at the wrong time. The situation is most serious, the way he uses Adam. He let Adam read the court papers. I can't count on him to pay Adam's medical bills. It is impossible to work anything out with him. It's always something."

Susan made the following proposal: John could see Adam every other weekend from after school on Friday to Sunday at 7:00 P.M.; one evening a week on the weeks he didn't have Adam for the weekend; one month in the summer; the last week of Christmas vacation; the first half of Easter vacation; Father's Day weekend; and on Adam's birthday every other year.

Adam's parents and I discussed the situation and focused on summer plans, since that was their most crucial concern at the time. Together we sketched out a plan and reviewed it with each parent's attorney and Adam's stepmother, all of whom were in the waiting room.

It was agreed that Adam would spend six weeks with his father that summer and the remainder of the vacation with his mother. The parent with whom Adam was not living would have him for one twenty-four-hour period each week. Adam's parents also agreed to return in two weeks to discuss a perma-

THE PROBlemes with
DIVOICes is They teare
into woars
                stop
                stop   THE
                        ↳counsler

MOM   DAD

                THE
                ↳children

nent parenting plan. I suggested they consider having Adam
spend alternate weekends with each of them from Friday after school through Monday morning and one evening every
week overnight.

John opened the next session by announcing adamantly,
"I want a restraining order against Susan dumping on Adam.

Susan told him everything that happened in court and when I picked him up from school the next day, he was mad at me."

Susan blurted out angrily, "He picked Adam up without telling me."

John continued, "Susan gave Adam a distorted idea of what went on. She laid a guilt trip on him. Adam cried because Susan doesn't have the time or money to plan fun things like I do."

Susan retorted, "It's difficult for me without money and Adam sees it. I have court expenses again and he [John] is not paying his bills."

Susan, John, and I discussed the situation. I told them that from where I sat I could see ways that both of them were dumping on Adam.

John said defensively, "I'm forced to counter her constant campaign of alienation against me, so I asked Adam, 'What does your mother pay for?' "

I explained to Susan and John how damaging it was for Adam to hear these negative remarks and to be pressured to take sides with one parent against the other. Adam's parents agreed to a mutual restraining order prohibiting them both from discussing financial issues with Adam and from making derogatory statements, including subtle negative comments in front of Adam. Afterward Susan said defensively, "I didn't tell Adam everything I could have."

The remainder of the session was used to discuss a parenting plan. John was now willing to have Adam on alternate weekends from Friday through Monday morning, and one evening a week overnight, but Susan still said, "No school nights!"

At this point I suggested they return for another session and bring Adam with them. From the way these parents were fighting, I knew Adam must be suffering greatly from their conflict, and I told them I felt it would be helpful and unburdening for Adam to come. They agreed to another session in a few weeks.

On the day of their appointment, Susan and John brought Adam to my office. I briefly explained to the child that the purpose of our meeting was to make things easier for him. I asked him if he would like to draw a picture or read a book while I talked with his parents. Adam took paper and crayons and settled down in the waiting room.

John announced that the summer schedule was working, and Susan said next year she wanted the vacation schedule to be planned ahead so she could enroll Adam for tennis lessons. We discussed this briefly, and I volunteered to help them work on it later. We went together to the waiting room, where Adam showed us a drawing he had made which clearly indicated the pain he was experiencing. His parents and I were deeply touched. There were tears in his parents' eyes.

I escorted Adam into my office, where I asked him what he thought was going on between his parents.

Adam replied, "One wants to do one thing, and the other wants to do another thing. They have big fights. My mom says bad things about my dad, and my dad says bad things about my mom. I don't know who to listen to."

I asked him how that made him feel, and he told me that it upset him, so that he felt bad all over.

I asked Adam how his living arrangement was working out and he told me that it was okay, but sometimes there was a problem "'cause of mixed-up plans." He described a situation that had occurred recently. "We were visiting my mom's sister. We came home and we were waiting for my dad but he didn't come. Finally my mother called my dad to see when he was coming and my dad said he thought that my mom was bringing me to his house. Later on I asked my dad about it and he told me that my mom was supposed to pick me up, but my mom said my dad was." Adam said that this had happened a few times.

I asked Adam, "How do you get along with your mother?" He replied, "Good, she's nice."

Then I asked Adam how he got along with his dad, and Adam said, "I get along good, except when I ask dad questions

that my mom asks me to ask him." He explained that made
his dad a little uptight and that in turn made him feel uncomfortable. He added, "Sometimes I think my dad is wrong but
he tries to convince me that he isn't."

At the end of our interview I asked Adam, "What would
you like to see happen now?" and he answered, "I'd like for
them to stop saying this and that about each other when I go
to each of their houses. I want them to stop getting mad at
each other on the phone."

When I asked Adam if he would give me permission to
tell his parents what we had talked about, Adam agreed. We
invited them in and they listened attentively. Then Susan and
John agreed to return once again to try to develop a parenting plan that could meet Adam's needs and reduce the
acrimony between them for their child's sake.

On the morning of our next appointment Susan came, but
John was late. We waited a few minutes for him, then I escorted Susan into my office, where she told me it was not
working out well. John, she said, was not cooperating. She told
me that he had kept Adam on her day off after he had agreed
not to. "He does as he pleases," she said. "What can I do? I
don't think he will even come today."

At this point I called John, who answered the phone sleep-
ily, "I thought our appointment was for 11:00 A.M." He
checked his calendar and apologized, and said he would arrive
in thirty minutes.

Meanwhile, Susan told me how touched she was by
Adam's drawing. "He has not verbalized this before. I decided
never to argue again in front of Adam, but John makes everything so difficult."

I suggested we work out a schedule so things could go
more smoothly between them and arguments could be avoided.
I suggested that she write John a note when she knew her
working schedule so that he could select days to see Adam
when she would be working, not on her days off.

Susan was still apprehensive, "When he doesn't return
Adam on my days, what recourse do I have?"

I told Susan that a good parenting plan would help them and help Adam. She continued to object to Adam spending any school nights with his father because: (1) John wouldn't cooperate about Adam's homework, and (2) John didn't return Adam's clothes.

I suggested to Susan that it was Adam's responsibility to do his homework, not hers, and that it was best in most cases for parents to allow their children to take this responsibility themselves. Susan told me that in general she agreed; however, Adam had had to repeat kindergarten and be tutored for a year and a half after that. Now it was too costly to continue with the tutoring, and although Adam was very bright, he was slow in doing his homework and needed a parent to supervise him every night. John would not take this responsibility and therefore she wanted Adam home on school nights so she could be sure he did his homework. Adam, she told me, was two years behind emotionally.

I told Susan bluntly that if the "war" between John and her didn't stop, Adam would be in a lot worse shape than he was. I also told her that I would be talking to John about this issue when he arrived, and perhaps he would also be willing to take some responsibility for supervising Adam.

Susan stated that she would be willing to give some of the responsibility for Adam's education to John, "But he agrees to anything and then he just won't cooperate."

At this point John arrived, and handed me a holiday chart that he had prepared. Both parents were in agreement about all the holidays except Christmas vacation; after some discussion they tentatively agreed to alternate the first and second halves of the vacation.

I then introduced a discussion about regular schedules throughout the year. I began by summarizing Susan's position and her concern about Adam spending school nights with the father. I asked John if he would be willing to take responsibility for sitting with Adam on certain school nights and helping him complete his homework assignments. John replied that he "would like to take some responsibility to do homework with

Adam." He also brought up the same idea that Susan and I had talked about earlier, namely, that Susan would send John a note two weeks in advance, listing the days she had to work. John would select weekdays to have Adam other than her days off. John said he liked that idea very much.

Both John and Susan asked me to help them draft an agreement that they could consider and discuss with their attorneys. They agreed to return in two weeks, at which time they would sign the agreement or make the necessary changes. The three of us drafted the following agreement:

1. The parents would continue to have joint legal custody of Adam.

2. During the school year, Adam would spend the following times with his father: alternate weekends from Friday, 3:00 P.M., to Monday, 8:30 A.M.; one evening each week, on Tuesdays or another evening on which the mother worked, from 3:00 P.M. overnight through the following morning at 8:30 A.M. Susan agreed to provide John with her schedule in writing two weeks in advance, or less, by mutual agreement.

3. Summer vacation schedule: Adam would spend the first part of summer vacation through August 1 with his mother on even years and with his father on odd years, and the other half with the other parent.

4. Holiday and vacation schedules:
   (a) Holidays for mother: Mother's Day, mother's birthday and the following holidays on even years: New Year's weekend from December 31 at 6:00 P.M. to noon the day before school begins; Martin Luther King's birthday, July 4, Thanksgiving Day, Lincoln's birthday, Columbus Day, Adam's birthday, the first part of Christmas vacation from the day school let out through December 26, 8:00 A.M., and the second half of Easter vacation.

(b) Holidays for father: every Father's Day and father's birthday and the following holidays on even years: Washington's birthday weekend, Memorial Day weekend, Labor Day weekend, Veterans' Day, the second half of Christmas vacation from December 26, 8:00 A.M. through December 31, 6:00 P.M., and the first part of Easter vacation. On odd years, they would switch.

5. The parents were restrained from arguing in front of Adam, from making derogatory statements about each other to Adam, and from pressuring Adam to take sides on disputed issues.

As they were leaving, each with a copy of the agreement, John said, "I never dreamed we would accomplish so much today. I just didn't expect it." I reminded both of them how happy Adam would be if they could settle their differences, but I could hear them arguing over who would pay for Adam's summer classes as they walked down the hall.

Susan and John spent most of the next session arguing over the issue of Adam spending Tuesday nights with John, Susan insisting he would lose too much sleep.

John was livid. His wife, Karen, put her head in her hands. John said, "I want more time with Adam. I'm not going to give up having Adam at least one night a week. I guess we're going to have to go to court."

I asked Susan to consider the possibility that this extra time with John might benefit Adam enough to outweigh his missing a little sleep, but she would not hear of it.

Then I asked them both to consider a compromise: Adam would stay overnight on Tuesday evenings only on the weeks his father did not have him for the weekend. On alternate Tuesdays John would return Adam by 9:00 P.M. John said he would agree to it and so did Susan.

All the issues they had raised had been resolved. Both Susan and John indicated that they were satisfied, and each left with a copy of the revised agreement. No further appointment was set. They would be in touch with me about their final decision after they discussed it with their attorneys.

The morning after our appointment John telephoned me. His attorney would be calling me, he said, about the informal wording of the agreement. Otherwise, he was prepared to sign it. However, John was upset because of an argument he had with Susan on the previous evening about who was to pick up and return Adam. I told him for Adam's sake these arguments had to stop. I suggested they come in again to discuss this and to smooth out some last rough spots. He accepted my suggestion gratefully.

While John was still on the phone, I telephoned Susan on another line. I told her that John was prepared to sign their agreement; Susan said she was too. I also told her that John had mentioned the argument of the night before, and I repeated what I had said to John, "These arguments have to stop." When I mentioned that John was willing to return to my office the following week to discuss this, if she would come, she accepted and warmly thanked me for all my help.

This would be our fifth meeting. If John and Susan could not reach an agreement this time, I would have to suggest a referral for continued family counseling elsewhere in the community. My motivation to help them learn to resolve their differences and cooperate regarding Adam was very strong. I knew Adam was counting on me.

Susan telephoned me the day before our appointment to change the date and I called John, who expressed deep frustration: "It's like pulling teeth. All the delays." He agreed to attend our next meeting, but said that if a final agreement was not reached this time he intended to go to court for a solution.

When John and Susan arrived for their appointment, I greeted them warmly and asked each of them what they hoped to accomplish that day. They both said, almost in unison, "To finalize our agreement."

However, John had some issues he wanted to raise. The first was that Susan share half the driving on weekends and vacations. Susan refused flatly. "That's ridiculous. I don't get home from work on Friday until 6:00 P.M. I'd have to give Adam dinner and I wouldn't be able to get him to your house until 9:00 P.M."

I pointed out to John that he would miss dinner with Adam if Susan brought Adam to him so late. After some thought, John decided to drop the issue.

He then asked to be able to make changes in his schedule should he have to go out of town on business and miss some of his days with Adam. Susan refused to have this in writing but indicated that she would try to accommodate him. I suggested the following formula, which both accepted: Should either parent find it necessary to miss an assigned evening, day, or weekend with Adam because of business commitments, the other parent would make every effort to allow him or her to make up the time missed as soon as possible.

The last issue John had on his agenda was the restraining order against making derogatory statements in Adam's presence. He and his attorney were requesting that Susan not contact any member of John's family.

Susan responded to this angrily, "I'm friendly with his parents and his sister. I won't be restrained from talking to them. He talks about me too."

They began to argue over this. After a few minutes I said, "I would like to remind you both why you are here—to make life easier for Adam. When either of you makes derogatory statements about the other, it keeps the war going, and that hurts Adam. He wants the war to end."

Susan nodded affirmatively, "It's Adam's birthday today."

"Wouldn't it be a wonderful birthday present for Adam if you could settle all this today?" I asked. Together we wrote the following restraining order: Parents are restrained from arguing with each other in front of Adam, and from making derogatory statements to anyone about the other parent in Adam's presence. Parents shall not discuss disputed issues with Adam or pressure him to take sides.

Now it was Susan's turn to present her agenda. The first issue dealt with the length of time that each parent could take

Adam away on vacation. Susan opted for three weeks, not six weeks as John had requested. She said, "If you want to keep him away longer, I'll probably agree."

John protested. He didn't like the idea of having to ask Susan's permission to keep Adam longer, and he insisted he wanted the six weeks' vacation in writing. After fifteen minutes of argument, I suggested they consider a four-week vacation with an additional two-week option by mutual agreement, consent not to be unreasonably withheld. When they could not agree on this, I suggested splitting the difference and making it twenty-five days. Neither of them liked this, and an impasse developed until Susan said, "Let's skip over this and come back to it later."

Susan then stated that plans must not be made between John and Adam without her knowledge. John had sometimes picked up Adam at school on her day and taken him to buy shoes or sports equipment without telling her. John agreed to telephone her and let her know beforehand. A statement was written incorporating this point.

The only issue still unresolved was that of summer vacation. I told them, "You have come a long way. If you can't resolve this issue here, I can write up all that you have agreed to, and you can ask the judge to decide on this one."

John yielded. "I'll settle on a one-month vacation with an option for six weeks, as you suggested," he said.

Susan yielded too: "Okay, I'll go for four weeks."

I spent the next thirty minutes writing up their agreement, while in a calm manner they discussed the anxiety Adam was experiencing in entering a new school and making new friends. "I like the way you are discussing Adam together," I told them. "This is the kind of cooperation and support he needs from both of you."

I gave each of them a copy of the agreement to read over carefully and show to their attorneys. I also gave Susan the original; after she signed it, she was to give it to John for his signature and he would return it to me. Both of them said I would be hearing from them within a few days.

A week went by and I discovered that what was holding up the signing were a few minor items, such as the wording of the paragraph pertaining to "missed" days.

I suggested an alternate wording and offered to meet with them again, but they preferred a conference phone call. The items in question were smoothed out in less than half an hour. John and Susan were to be in court two days later for their financial hearing, and they came to my office that morning to sign their agreement.

Hallelujah! I told the two of them, "This is a real triumph for you. It shows how much you both care about Adam." I wished them well, and commended the two attorneys for their assistance.

How these parents will get along in the future is yet to be seen. This is a great concern of mine, but I firmly believe that the parenting agreement they signed will help keep things running more smoothly for them and for Adam.

As this true story illustrates, a possessive attitude on the part of either parent causes children pain. It can lead to parents' competing with one another, pulling, tugging, and pressuring a child, and even kidnapping the children. A child in the middle of such a conflict feels insecure and powerless, trapped in the position of having to choose between parents, tormented by self-hatred and guilt. The longer the parental conflict and competition last, the more pain for the child and the greater the chance that the child's self-esteem will suffer. This, in turn, will reduce his or her chances for happiness, fulfillment and success.

Instead of competing, parents can share in raising their children. There is plenty of work and responsibility to go around. There is no scarcity of things to do for growing children and usually no really valid reason for one parent to try to have sole responsibility.

Without help, Adam's parents might have gone on competing and fighting indefinitely. If you as a parent find yourself caught in an ongoing battle, or even continual, subtle disagreements over the children, I strongly suggest that you seek divorce mediation and/or divorce counseling that includes the other parent.

If the other parent refuses to participate, seek help on your own. It will benefit you personally to learn how to approach and deal with the other parent, and this can make a positive difference for your children. Often, even small changes made by one parent can defuse the situation and bring much needed relief from tension and despair.

5

Rebuilding a Support System for Your Child

A child's universe is shaken when parents separate and divorce. In many cases, in addition to the changes that occur naturally during a separation, important family members disappear from children's lives. It could be a father or a mother, grandparents, a stepparent, an aunt or uncle or cousin, or a close family friend. One entire side of a child's family may suddenly become unavailable because of parental competition and anger.

The loss of special family members and important relationships is extremely painful and damaging for children, for they need a family. They also need love, support, and reassurance from many special people, particularly at such a time. For their children's sake, parents should make every effort to preserve and foster all of a child's familial relationships no matter how angry or upset they may be with the other parent and the other parent's family.

Realistically—and ideally—when a marriage or a relationship ends, it is not the end of the family for the children who are involved. The form and structure of the child's family change. Instead of a mother and father together, with family and friends from both sides, the child has two separate parents, along with each parent's family and friends. In time, stepparents—and their families—may become important additions to the child's family. All these people constitute the child's restructured family and are an important support network for the child. It is vital that the child have these people available.

The fewer losses a child sustains after separation or divorce, the greater are the chances for healing to take place and for feelings of security and well-being to come about.

The two configurations on page 71 illustrate visually the way in which the structure of a child's family changes after divorce, yet all family members remain available to the child.

Grandparents, relatives, and close family friends should be asked by each parent not to make derogatory remarks about the other parent in the child's presence, not to pressure the child to take sides against the other parent, and not to pump the child for information regarding the other parent. They should not question the children as to where they want to live, or discuss legal, financial, or custody issues with the children. All family members should be made to understand that this will harm the children.

Parents who have had a falling-out with their former in-laws and relatives during the marriage or since the divorce should try to defuse the tension. This will help avoid family feuds and future problems for the children.

Debbie, a young mother, told me that she had never liked her mother-in-law: "She interfered in our marriage. She'd talk to Chris (Debbie's former husband) about things but not to me. I don't want her picking up my baby. If Chris can't come and get him, she can't have him. I could be as nice as pie and let her have him, but I won't."

In a frustrated voice, Chris said, "Debbie, you're not being fair. When I get off work a little late, I need her to pick up the baby. *Your* mother watches the baby while *you* work. I'll go to court if I have to."

I told both parents that if they want their child to feel secure, they should both be "as nice as pie" for her sake. I pointed out to them that they had a long time ahead of them during which they needed to work together.

Nevertheless, each of them held strongly to his or her position and would not budge. They went to court over this issue, and one can only imagine what grief lies ahead for their baby.

Child's Family Structure Before Divorce

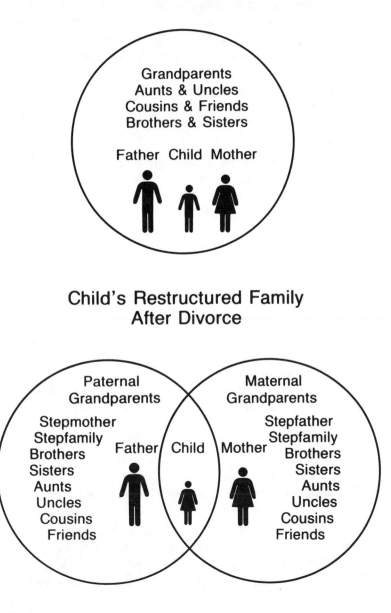

Grandparents
Aunts & Uncles
Cousins & Friends
Brothers & Sisters

Father   Child   Mother

Child's Restructured Family After Divorce

Paternal
Grandparents

Maternal
Grandparents

Stepmother
Stepfamily
Brothers
Sisters
Aunts
Uncles
Cousins
Friends

Father   Child   Mother

Stepfather
Stepfamily
Brothers
Sisters
Aunts
Uncles
Cousins
Friends

A Message to Unwed Parents

Whenever possible, unwed fathers should be given access to their child and be included in the child's life. The plight of children of unwed parents is especially sensitive and fragile. Many such children grow up without remembering or ever getting to see or know their father. Now many unwed fathers who want to be involved in their child's life are reaching out to establish their rights as parents. When unwed mothers refuse to acknowledge them as the father, or refuse access to the child, unwed fathers may find it necessary to go to court to establish their rights legally.

Some of these unwed fathers experience tremendous pain and frustration in trying to see their children, especially if they cannot afford an attorney, and many give up. James, a young unwed father in his early twenties, was in such a predicament. He walked into my office one day and asked for help in order to see his three-year-old son. He told me that he and his son's mother, Lynn had lived together for several years but had never married, and that they had separated six months before. With great emotion James said, "Lynn is completely unwilling to let me see my son. Every time I try to see him, she threatens to call the police." He broke down and wept. "This has been so hard for me."

When I suggested that he consider seeking legal advice in order to establish himself as the father and to obtain visitation rights, he explained that he was unemployed and could not afford an attorney. I asked James if he had tried to get help through Legal Aid, and he said that he had applied to Legal Aid but was told they did not take this kind of case; it was they who had referred him to me for help.

I told James that I was willing to telephone Lynn and ask if she would agree to come to my office to discuss the situation. He enthusiastically accepted my offer. While James waited outside, I called Lynn and identified myself as a counselor in the conciliation court. I told her that James was seeking to obtain visitation rights to see his child. Lynn became very upset and said, "James can't see my child. I want nothing to do with him, and if he ever comes around here, I will call the police."

I asked her if she would be willing to come to my office and meet with James and me. She was very negative at first, but after we talked for a while she finally agreed to attend a conference. I brought James back into my office at this point and, and with Lynn on the phone, set up a mutually agreeable appointment.

On the day of the appointment Lynn and James were both present, but she was extremely negative about James having any contact with their child. I told her all the things I say to parents regarding the needs of children and the importance of a child having contact with both parents, but everything I said fell on deaf ears and she walked out.

I then suggested to James that he contact a fathers' rights group for assistance in establishing paternity and filing for visitation rights. I gave him the names of several groups, and he thanked me profusely and left.

It turned out that he would have to join a group to receive any kind of help, but the fee was forty dollars and he did not have the money. I suggested that he go to the law library to do research on how to file the papers himself. Within a few minutes he was back with the information that there were no prepared forms for filing a paternity action. This did not sound right to me, so I walked James down the hall to the library and asked the law librarian myself. She confirmed what she had told James, and said he would have to make up his own form. This would involve buying legal paper at a stationery store, and then doing research on how to write up the "Order to Show Cause" to describe his situation and his request.

I took James downstairs to the county clerk's office and again asked about paternity action forms. The file clerk confirmed that indeed such forms did not exist, and that anyone wishing to file a paternity action had to seek legal advice or prepare the papers themselves. James said he could barely read and write, so the situation seemed hopeless: James could not afford legal advice, and he did not have the knowledge, skills, or education to be able to prepare his own legal case. He told me, "I'm going to give up. My son will have to grow up without a father unless Lynn changes her mind." He walked out of the door in tears, and I felt sad for his son to see him go.

Unwed mothers like Lynn, who exclude their child's father, may be setting their children up for feelings of rejection, abandonment, and lifelong unhappiness. One adorable three-year-old, Bianca, who had never seen her father, would go up to every man she saw and ask, "Are you my daddy?" She might have gone on looking for her daddy her whole life long, had I not been able to convince her mother, Dana, that Bianca had a right to know who her father was. I also told her that someday Bianca might be very angry when she found out that her mother had kept her away from her father.

Dana took this advice to heart and within two weeks called me to arrange a meeting between her and Bianca's father, Gino, to discuss his visiting Bianca. Gino lived in another state, and Dana had not seen him since Bianca's birth. That meeting was extremely difficult for her, for she was still enraged at him "for letting Bianca and me down before her birth, after he'd promised to help me." Gino had not wanted to be a father, and had changed his mind at the last minute and run away. Dana was left alone at a most difficult time, and she was not prepared to forgive Gino for that. When Bianca was a few months old, Dana took her baby and moved away, determined to raise her daughter alone. When Gino tried periodically to see Bianca, Dana refused him access. She was concerned that he would let Bianca down "the way he did me."

During their meeting Dana asked Gino what his intentions were toward her daughter. Was he going to make a commitment to see her regularly? If not, he couldn't see her at all. Gino told her he wanted to be Bianca's father. He apologized for his past behavior and offered to give Dana money for Bianca every month. Dana agreed that the father could see Bianca the following month, but in the meantime, she wanted to prepare Bianca for his visit.

When the time came, Dana told me, "Gino walked in.

Bianca looked at him, walked all the way around him, looked him straight in the eyes very seriously and said, 'You hurt my mommy and me. Why did you do it?' Tears came into Gino's eyes and he told her how sorry he was for what he had done. He gave her a little gift he had brought for her. She opened it. A big smile lit up her face. She took his hand and led him into her room where they played with her toys for an hour and a half."

Gino has visited Bianca every few months since and calls her once a week. On her fifth birthday, both of Bianca's parents took her to Disneyland for the day. Dana describes Bianca's behavior as less restless and irrational since she has been seeing her father. Before that she often woke up in the night screaming inconsolably and thrashing about in anger. That behavior has stopped. Fortunately, Dana was willing to reconsider her former decision, go through this pain from the past, and give her daughter a father.

A Message to Stepparents

If you married a man or woman with a child, you inherited a stepchild and that child's entire family. You are now an important part of this family too, even if it may appear otherwise to you. Your stepchildren may be giving you a difficult time. They may be struggling with feelings of disloyalty to the other parent, and as a result may resist loving you. They could actually be under pressure from the other parent not to accept you or enjoy you, or on their own they could be blaming you for the divorce or for taking a parent away from them. The other parent may be feeling threatened by your presence and may be causing you problems. And there are other family members to deal with and many sensitive issues to handle. At times, all of these problems may seem insurmountable.

Your patience, understanding, and kindness can help your stepchild adjust to you, and can ultimately help you and your spouse have a closer relationship. The more you can deescalate conflict between your spouse and the other parent, and the better you get along with your stepchild, the more comfortable and happy your own marriage will be.

The following case demonstrates the strain and pressure placed on a marriage when love and support are not forthcoming from a stepparent.

Bonnie and George had been married two years after living together for six years. It was a second marriage for both of them and they each had one child. After the marriage, Bonnie's ten-year-old son lived with them. George's eighteen-year-old daughter Jill lived with her mother, and was now living with her husband of one year.

Bonnie was thinking of separating from George because of their problems over Jill, which began even before they were married. Bonnie came in alone to see me for counseling, and began angrily, "Three years ago, George forced me to have Jill live with us. We only had a small apartment and we were very crowded. I said no, but he brought her in anyway." She explained that this had occurred just after Jill had dropped out of high school. George had been very concerned about her and had planned to enroll her in a special school near their home. She continued, "His plan didn't work out because Jill wouldn't get up for school and it was an awful situation. I asked both of them to leave. George and I were separated for a while, then we got back together."

Then the year before, Bonnie and George had argued over financing Jill's wedding. Bonnie told me, "I was shocked when I found out how much it would cost. We didn't have that kind of money. George told me he wouldn't pay more than $2,500, but I knew it would go way over that. And that's the way it is even now—I just can't trust him to keep his word. He goes behind my back to do things for Jill. The last straw was his giving Jill the bed he bought for her when she moved in with us. I told him no, but he gave it to her anyway. He ignores my feelings. I can't depend on him to make me his first priority." Bonnie said that when she confronted George about the bed he told her that he couldn't stand the stress, so he gave the bed to Jill. "It's easier for him to say no to me than to Jill," she said.

Power struggles and stresses of this kind are deadly to a marriage. Even if a stepparent should "win," he or she loses. A stepparent should avoid placing the natural parent in the position of having to choose between the stepparent and his or her own children. In most cases, the children "win," because the bond that exists between a parent and child is so strong. Trying to come between a parent and child is like trying to hold back a mighty river.

When I explained this to Bonnie, she, having a child of her own, understood what I was saying. She had erroneously expected George to put her needs before his daughter's, and when he didn't, she was furious. It is wise and helpful for stepparents to join forces with the natural parent in caring for children, rather than tear the natural parent apart inside. The more compassion and support stepparents can give to their stepchildren, the more love they are likely to get from their new husband or wife.

Many stepparents play primary roles in raising their stepchildren, especially in cases where their spouse has primary custody or joint custody. To them, I wish to emphasize the importance of encouraging stepchildren to maintain a positive relationship with the other parent. A stepmother or stepfather doing this would be acting in the best interests of the stepchildren and ultimately in his or her own. The reason is that the stepchildren will feel better about themselves and have fewer problems, and the spouse will be happier and freer to enjoy his or her new marriage.

The following case is that of a boy raised by his father and stepmother since he was two. He is now fifteen. Jeff's parents divorced when he was a year old. He lived with his mother, Carolyn, until he was three. Then Carolyn felt unable to care for him, because she was going through a difficult time emotionally and she thought Jeff would be better off with his father, Andrew, and his new stepmother, Monica. Carolyn told me that almost immediately Monica took over the role of Jeff's mother and squeezed Carolyn out of Jeff's life. For example, Monica had Jeff call her "mommy." After being refused access to Jeff time after time, Carolyn "ran away," because the pain and frustration became too much for her to deal with. Periodically, she would call and be hung up on, or drop by to see Jeff when she came to town but would still be refused access. It took her years to save the money to take Andrew to court for visitation rights. By this time Jeff was so angry at her for having abandoned him he did not want to see her.

Meanwhile, Jeff was having serious learning and behavioral problems at school, and was eventually placed in a school for emotionally disturbed children. I met with the entire family and encouraged Monica and Andrew to help their son establish a relationship with Carolyn. They reluctantly agreed, provided Jeff wanted a relationship with his mother.

When I spoke to Jeff, who regarded me sullenly, he said, "I'm afraid to give Carolyn a chance. She might run out on me again and then I might mess up again at school. She didn't want me. She just wanted to do her own thing. That was more important to her. I'd like to get to know her, but I'm not sure how I'd feel. Maybe I'd screw up again. I don't want to get upset. I'd love to see her, but I'm worried. How will I react? I'm doing better at school now. I want it to stay the same. I'd like things to stay the same and be able to see her."

I told Jeff he was older now, and stronger; he could stand up for himself. I encouraged him to begin seeing Carolyn for short visits, to talk to her on the telephone every week, and see how that went. The next week he called Carolyn and they arranged to meet for lunch; Jeff then agreed to meet her once a week for dinner. He told her he was worried about how Monica would take it, but that regardless, he wanted to see Carolyn.

Children need the freedom to enjoy and love all members of their family. Jeff need not have suffered the way he did, had his stepmother been wiser and more understanding.

As a stepparent, you can help keep peace by not competing with the other parent, by reassuring your opposite that he or she is respected as the child's parent, and by telling the other person that you only want to be helpful and are not trying to usurp his or her position. This approach will pay off in many ways.

Stepparents can benefit from reading books on stepparenting. There are also stepparenting groups available in some areas, as well as family counseling agencies and divorce mediation centers where help can be found.

A Message to Grandparents

You are extremely important to your grandchild. There is no one who can give a child an ego boost quite as well as a doting grandparent can. It might be of interest to note that in California a bill was recently passed making it possible for grandparents to seek visitation rights in court.

Your grandchildren need your love, support, and protection. I say protection because some grandparents take sides and add to the tension caused by divorce by speaking ill of their former daughter- or son-in-law in front of their grandchild. This makes children very uncomfortable.

One little girl told me sadly, "I don't want to see my grandma anymore. She always says bad things about my mommy. It makes me feel bad. I wish she would stop."

Divorce is heartbreaking for grandparents, but in spite of your own disappointment and sadness, your help is needed to make peace for your grandchild's sake. You can help your grandchild by promoting peace between his or her parents and encouraging your grandchild to remain neutral. In addition, you can be a calming influence and offer as much help to both parents as you can. You will be doing this for your grandchild out of love, and also bringing some peace of mind to yourself.

6

Creating a Closer Relationship with Your Child

Even the best of parents make mistakes. I certainly have. You and I learned how to be parents from our own parents, and they in turn learned from their parents. So if mistakes are made, who can we blame? And, really, what good does it do to blame anybody? It is the responsibility of each of us to create the best possible situation and outcome for our children, and to interact with them in a way that will allow a close, loving relationship to develop. Children desperately need this closeness with both parents, even if they say they do not want to see one of them.

If you want your child to do well in life, the best gift you can give him or her is a close, loving relationship with you. The twelve guidelines below can help you achieve this closeness and make your child feel loved:

1. *Become a good listener.* Even if you don't agree with what your child is saying, be willing to listen without interrupting and then discuss the problem afterward. This will enable your child to feel he or she can talk to you.

2. *Allow your child to express feelings*, even hostile, angry feelings, and allow him or her to cry. This will help your child feel comfortable around you.

3. *Comfort and reassure your child* when he or she is upset. This will establish feelings of security and of being loved by you.

4. *Be demonstrative—show your affection for your child.* Be free with your hugs and kisses and, whenever appropriate, tell your child that you love him or her. This will establish a loving closeness between you.

5. *Protect your child from parental disputes or disagreements.* If you involve the child, it will make him or her feel insecure and uncomfortable around you.

6. *Set reasonable rules and limits for your child's behavior according to his or her age and development.* In time this will help him or her to see you as fair and reasonable. It is not unusual for young children to have temper tantrums when they do not get their way. They should be allowed to cry, kick, or scream without either being punished for it or given their way. Gradually your child will learn your rules and what behavior you expect.

7. *Along with discipline, give your children as much praise as you can.* This will help them grow up feeling good about themselves. Avoid corporal punishment of any kind: slapping, grabbing, hitting, beating, shaking, choking, or any action that might make your child fear you. Harsh punishment can weaken your child's ego and destroy your chances for a close relationship. Avoid threatening to punish your child or threatening to send him or her away. Also avoid prolonged punishments, such as long periods of being grounded or deprived of privileges.

8. *Do not call your child names or use put-downs.* These can cause the child to feel unloved, uneasy and insecure.

It may also make him or her overly sensitive and, in later life, spoil his or her capacity to have fun with friends.

9. *Set realistic goals for your child,* and try not to have unrealistic expectations based on what *you* wanted out of life. Do not make your child feel guilty over disappointing you, for this could make him or her feel like a bad person and become uncomfortable or sad in your presence.

10. *Avoid excessive behavior,* especially drug use and alcohol abuse around your child. If you have a drinking or drug abuse problem, be honest with yourself about your habit or addiction and get help for yourself. Children become very frightened when parents are high or out of control. Your child will dread being around you and eventually will not want to see you at all.

11. *Spend some leisure time and play with your child.* Choose activities geared to your child's age and interests. There is a wide variety of activities that children enjoy: picnics, walks, biking, simple games, and cooking. There are also inexpensive places to take children, such as parks, beaches, or museums, and occasionally including one of your child's friends can increase the enjoyment. Avoid activities for young children that involve long periods of sitting.

12. Gradually, patiently, and with love, help your child to learn and grow in knowledge, skills, and independence as he or she is ready. The better your child feels about himself or herself, the better he or she will feel about you.

Parenting After the Divorce

The guidelines above are basic for developing closer parent-child relationships in general. I have given some additional thoughts below for divorcing parents. These can minimize the risk of your child feeling abandoned, caught in the middle or helpless, and of you losing the trust, love and affection of your child.

See your child as soon as possible after the separation

If parents decide to separate, arrangements should be made for the children to see and spend time with each parent as soon as possible. Many children feel very anxious when a parent moves out of the home. They should be taken as soon as possible to visit the parent's new home and should be given a telephone number so they can contact their father or mother whenever they feel the need to do so.

Some young children feel very guilty when their parents separate, believing that in some unexplained way they caused the divorce. We might find this a strange or unusual reaction but it happens frequently. They need to be told that the divorce is not because of them, and be given reassurance that the parent who leaves will not disappear from their lives. They can be reassured by words like, "Mommy [or daddy] and I are not going to live together anymore, but I will still see you a lot [or "whenever I can," or "on Sundays or weekends"]. I will be calling you to say hello and find out how you are doing. I love you and I will always be your mommy [or daddy]." A few simple words like these will let your child know that he or she is not losing you.

Despite such reassurance, some children will continue to feel insecure. Such children will test their parents to make sure they are still loved and won't be cast aside, for often they fear that their parents may divorce them, too. They may misbehave to put parents to the test. Although parents may become exasperated at such behavior, they should avoid threatening to send the children away, or saying, "I don't want you here anymore!" It is far more helpful for parents to be firm and tell the children to stop what they are doing, while letting them know at the next opportunity that they still love them. A combination of firmness and affection lets children know that their parents will not abandon them, but that they will set reasonable limits for the children's behavior.

Encourage your child to have a positive relationship with the other parent

One parent's relationship with a child is not enough, and a relationship with a stepparent cannot make up for the loss of a parent. Since young children do not understand adult problems or situations, when they become estranged from a parent they experience this as *not* being loved, or as being forgotten, ignored, neglected, rejected, or abandoned. They tend to blame themselves and feel unlovable. They think to themselves, *If I were worth loving, then my daddy (or mommy) would love me and want to be with me. Since my daddy (or mommy) doesn't see me or spend time with me, it must be because I am not worth loving.* These negative feelings tend to diminish a child's chances for success and happiness.

For this reason, if no other, in addition to nurturing your own relationship with your child, I suggest you encourage your child to have a positive relationship with the other parent as well. You will be promoting that relationship for the sake of your child, not for the other parent.

The following case demonstrates the great unhappiness that can be caused by trying to punish a former spouse.

Mark and Chris were only one and three years old respectively when their parents separated. It was their mother, Margie, who left their father, Jim, "to get away from Jim's domineering and controlling ways." Margie told me that she left the boys with Jim because she couldn't see how she could possibly support them. A few months later she found a job and wanted to take the children, but Jim wouldn't talk to her or allow her to see the boys. She found an attorney and took Jim to court, where he was awarded custody and Margie was given visitation rights on alternate weekends and alternate holidays.

Jim reluctantly complied with the court order but he kept the battle going. He was extremely bitter toward Margie for leaving him and the children, and he let his sons know it.

Four years later, in an attempt to obtain custody of her sons, Margie took Jim to court again. I met with the two of them in the conciliation court at that time, but when the situation was not resolved, a custody investigation was ordered. The investigator recommended that the children remain with Jim and that Margie have liberal visitation rights.

Margie tried to get custody of the children again six years later. This time I met with both the parents and the children. Mark was now thirteen and Chris was eleven. Before interviewing the children, I first conferred with the parents. With great emotion Margie told me, "Jim is constantly trying to turn the boys against me. His bitterness has increased since my remarriage. I want full custody so he won't turn them against me. He can see them on alternate weekends."

Jim replied angrily, "I've had the boys since they were babies. She left them and now she wants them back. The investigator recommended that they remain with me. When she left she talked about putting them in a foster home, so I took them. I can't stand a mother who would give her kids away."

I talked to Jim and Margie about how hard conflicts of this kind are on children, especially when they continue over a period of years. My concern appeared to fall on deaf ears. Then I asked to speak to each of the boys alone. Chris volunteered to go first. I ushered him into my office.

I asked Chris, "What do you think is going on between your parents?"

Chris answered, "It's bad. My mom wants to be friends, but my dad don't—because my mom left us."

I asked Chris how his parents' conflict made him feel and he replied, "I feel uncomfortable and nervous." He said that this had been going on for ten years.

I then asked Chris, "How do you feel about your mother leaving you when you were little?"

Chris replied, "Pretty bad." I asked, "Why do you think she left you?"

He answered, "Probably when we were little we couldn't do no work for her. Now we could."

When I asked Chris, "Do you think your mother loves you?" he answered, "She loves me a little bit." He added, "The man across the street told me that my mom was filthy. He's very honest."

I asked Chris, "What would you like to see happen now?"

Chris replied, "I want my mom and dad to get along and no more fighting."

I thanked him for talking to me and got his permission to share what we talked about with his parents.

Mark was next, and he told me, "My dad doesn't want to talk to my mom, but she wants to talk to him. Our neighbor agrees with my dad, because she didn't want us. I was three."

I asked Mark if he remembered living with his mother. He said, "I can't remember, but my dad told us she didn't want us. My mom said she didn't have any money to have us. My dad says, 'Go ask the neighbor.' My mom says he's lying. I don't know what to believe."

I asked, "How does all this make you feel?"

Mark replied, "I feel sad about the divorce and I feel bad my mom left us."

When I asked Mark if he believed his mother loves him, he answered, "Now I think she cares about us, but not before." He said he had a bad feeling about her leaving, "but she probably had a good reason. I don't believe anyone would just do something like that. Now she wants us back. My dad says she's unfit. I don't think she'll get us."

Mark showed me a notarized letter he wrote for the court

and stated, "My dad wanted me to write it. I don't like to write what my mom or dad do wrong. It makes me feel bad." The letter written by Mark stated: "I want to live with my father. He has always taken care of me. My mother never wanted us. She wanted us put in a foster home."

After the children's interview, I talked with Jim alone. We discussed his anger and bitterness and the way it was affecting his sons. Jim agreed to stop bad-mouthing Margie in front of his sons.

I told Jim, "Good. It's time to end the war."

I asked Jim what his own growing-up had been like, and he told me that he had left home at thirteen after his mother abandoned him to an alcoholic stepfather who beat him with a belt. Jim had not forgiven his own mother for leaving him, and he was not willing to allow his sons to feel loved by their mother either.

Children who suffer from feelings of abandonment tend to have low self-esteem, which they carry with them into adulthood. Jim is a good example of such a person, and of the way that unhappiness is transmitted from one generation to another. He has transmitted the pain he experienced as a child to his sons. If no change occurs for the better, his sons will in turn pass it on to their children.

This case is a prime and tragic example of the pain and damage done to many children of divorce. Because of Chris' assumption that his mother did not want him or love him, he will undoubtedly feel less worthwhile, less loved, and be less likely to succeed in life.

Jim could have spared his children ten years of pain. He could have tried to correct and normalize the situation a month after the separation, before this tremendous psychological harm was done to his sons. But Jim was thinking of his own disappointment and the pain of losing Margie, and not of what his sons needed. If he had been thinking of his sons, he would have encouraged Margie to spend as much time with the boys as she could. He would have been willing to communicate with her about the children and to cooperate in working out a schedule with her which would have allowed both of them to be involved in raising their children.

Instead, he took an already painful situation and made it much worse. He made the boys feel all the more abandoned, rejected, and unloved by constantly reminding them that their mother had left them and did not want them. He went so far as to involve a neighbor to back him up. In short, Jim allowed his own bitterness against Margie to ruin his sons' chances for a good life.

Jim also paid a price for holding on to his bitterness all those years. Holding grudges saps a person's energy and vitality and in the end brings little satisfaction. The questions one should ask oneself are: Is it worth holding on to my anger? Is it worth sacrificing my own life and the lives of my children?

In this case, Margie left her home and children, and Jim continued to punish her for this. More often it is the father who leaves the family at the time of separation, and it is the mother who wants to punish the father for leaving, by not cooperating in setting up schedules for the father to spend time with the children.

It is essential that parents get off to a good start when they decide to separate, or at least very soon thereafter. Parents should make every effort to correct a bad situation, or they will be storing up terrible and endless misery for themselves and their children.

See your child regularly

Children need regular visits. It is through frequent, ongoing contact that your child will feel loved and cared for. The younger the child, the more frequent your visits should be. Some parents put off seeing their children because they are "too busy" making a living or building a new life, or are too preoccupied with their own survival. Their children are not their main priority at this time. These parents may believe that at another time they will be able to spend more time with their children, without realizing that when that time comes, their children may not want to see them. The parents' preoccupation may have left their child feeling hurt and rejected, and in order to protect themselves from this pain, they may reject that parent in return.

If you are a parent who lives far away from your child and cannot see him or her often, there are ways of keeping in touch. Plan to see your child as often as you can. Even sporadic visits are better than no visits at all. One of the worst feelings a child may have to deal with is that of having been forgotten, rejected, and abandoned by a parent. Phone calls, thoughtful cards, notes, and small gifts will help your child feel loved.

Gain your child's trust

To your child, security means being able to count on both parents. Promises made to children should be kept in order to build and keep their trust.

Billy, a five-year-old, waited in the driveway of his mother's residence one Friday afternoon. He had his bag packed for the weekend and was anxiously looking out for his father, who had promised to pick him up at 5:00 P.M. At 6:00 P.M., his mother called to Billy to come in because it was getting dark. Billy refused to go into the house. "Daddy will come. He told me he would." At 6:30 P.M., he came into the house sobbing with disappointment. His father hadn't come and hadn't called. His mother had to hold Billy for an hour to calm him down.

Disappointments such as these undermine a child's security. Once a child loses trust in a parent, it is difficult to rebuild it. Parents should not make promises to their children that they cannot keep. If children can't trust their parents, whom can they trust?

When plans must be changed or canceled, call beforehand and notify the other parent. It is best also to speak to the child about this. A simple explanation can be very reassuring, such as: "I can't come tomorrow to pick you up. I am sick [or "I have to work," or "I'll be out of town," for example]. I am sorry, because I'll miss you. I'll be coming to pick you up on Sunday [or next week]. I love you. I'll see you then [or soon, or on Wednesday]."

If a parent is going to be late to pick up the children, he or she should make a telephone call to let them know. This will keep children from waiting and worrying. These small acts of consideration can help to spare children hours and days of feeling rejected.

Don't try to turn your child against the other parent

Barbara and Alan, divorcing parents of two teenage daughters, were ordered to talk to me when they were in court fighting over their children. Their attorneys spoke to me first and warned me that Barbara was making it difficult for the girls to see Alan or even talk to them because of her anger regarding Alan's girlfriend.

I escorted the two parents into my office and left their two daughters in the waiting room. Barbara began to tell me that Alan's girlfriend, Julie, had been in a fight with her older daughter Pamela, age sixteen, and slapped her. She insisted that Alan see his daughters alone and not with Julie. She stated, "Julie has no right to touch my child." With an angry look at Alan, she said, "The girls are very upset about Alan's unfaithfulness."

Alan began, "I grew up without a father. My father was always busy working. I spent a lot of time with my children. We were very close. I miss this close relationship now. I've been very depressed. I feel abandoned by them. Barbara has threatened to turn them away from me." Tears welled up in his eyes. "I feel sad and guilty about leaving them and about not being close." He said that he had left Barbara twice before because of all the arguments. "Our marriage was never right. We got married because Barbara was pregnant." Alan said he wasn't willing to exclude Julie when he had his daughters with him. When I asked him about the fight between Julie and Pamela, Alan said, "Pamela was mean to Julie because of all the bad things Barbara tells her about Julie and me."

They exchanged angry words for a few minutes. Then I spoke to them about the importance of them not transmitting any more of their anger and pain to their daughters and took took them back the waiting room.

Pamela came in and told me that her parents argued constantly over money, bills, and custody. When I asked her how that made her feel, she replied, "It makes me feel [pause] like, Why can't they settle everything and not just keep fighting. It upsets me because my mother takes her anger out on me. She screams at me and there is a lot of fighting going on in the house because of her anger." Pamela said that at times she felt very confused and had severe headaches. She said she saw her father whenever he was available and she could make it, but that, her mother questioned her incessantly about her father and his girlfriend. "It makes me feel very uncomfortable. I can't see my father without being questioned. I dread going back to her house and being questioned. She doesn't want me to see my dad."

I asked Pamela how she got along with her father and Julie, and she answered, "I get along fine with my dad and fine with Julie off and on. We have some arguments, usually about my dad spending money on me, otherwise its fine." I asked her if it was all right for Julie to be there when she was with her father and she said, "Yes." Pamela's idea about what caused the fight between her and Julie was that "Julie tries to run his life and tell him what to do—about buying me things, but later we talked about it and now it is fine, off and on."

When I asked Pamela what she wanted to see happen she replied, "Just to get the divorce over and get everything settled. I want both my parents to be happy. I want to continue living with my mom as long as everything goes well, and I'd like to see my dad twice or three times a week."

Next I interviewed Pamela's fifteen-year-old sister, Andrea. Andrea told me, "There's a lot of unnecessary hostility and acting foolish. They just fight and argue about little things and about money. It upsets me and makes me think how stupid it is for them do that. It make me feel pressured."

I asked her where she felt that pressure in her body and she said, "I feel it in my head and in my heart. It's frustration and pressure—kind of a pain. I feel love for both of my parents."

Andrea said that she and her mother got along fairly well: "We have some arguments about me cleaning up—the basics. We haven't had any arguments recently about me seeing my dad, just her comments. I don't blame her in a way. Dad has money and we don't." Andrea said she and her father got along well, but that she had never liked Julie. "My mom wouldn't want us to like her. It's my choice though."

I asked her if she thought that liking Julie would be a betrayal of her mother, and she answered, "It would be like betraying my mom right now, but not later on. I understand why my mom feels hurt. I try to make her feel better. I hug and kiss her in the morning to make her feel better."

Regarding her father, Andrea said, "I want to see him once on the weekend and once during the week and on special occasions. I hope it will be okay with my mom for me to see my dad. I'd see him anyway. He's still my father." She said there were certain things she could talk to her father about just as there were other things she preferred discussing with her mother.

She ended our talk by saying, "I want the divorce thing to be fair and for them to be friends."

I then brought the whole family together for a conference. At one point Barbara blurted out to her daughters, "You know I hate your father and wish he were dead."

I told Barbara, "You're feeling a lot of hurt, anger, and hatred toward Alan right now. Do you love your girls?"

Barbara replied, "I love them more than my own life."

"I know you love them," I responded, "but do you love them enough to want to spare them any more pain? This has been very hard on them. They have been experiencing a lot of strain and pain and they need relief. Are you willing to stop questioning them and stop making negative comments about their father and Julie in front of them? Are you willing to do this for them?"

Barbara looked down. Then she nodded her head affirmatively and said, "Yes." As they left, I could only hope that Barbara would be firm in her resolution for the sake of her girls.

Do not pressure your child to choose where he or she wants to live

One of the most painful and confusing situations to a child is to be asked to choose between the mother and the father. This causes a child to feel extremely insecure, especially when the issue of where he or she is going to live remains unresolved.

Tracy's parents had been quarreling over custody of Tracy since she was two years old. They came to see me when she was twelve. When I asked her how their constant fighting over her made her feel, she replied sadly, "I wish I were never born. Then they wouldn't have to fight."

Randy, a ten-year-old boy, who had lived with his mother since his parents separated three years before, said he felt extremely uncomfortable when his father asked him to live with him. "I was afraid to tell him I wanted to stay with my mom. I was afraid he'd be mad at me. I didn't know what to tell him, so I didn't say anything. I didn't want to hurt him."

It is evident that these children are unhappy under the burden their parents have placed upon them. Children should not have to endure this kind of pain.

Avoid discussion with your child of legal and financial matters pertaining to the divorce

Children have enough problems dealing with the emotional aspects of divorce and all the changes in their lives brought about by divorce. They don't need the extra burden of being told all the details of the court case.

When I interview children, some of them tell me of statements their parents have made. One six-year-old girl told me angrily, "My daddy is making it hard for my mommy. He wants to sell the house. Then we won't have any place to live." A fourteen-year-old boy said, "I feel like an attorney. My mom tells me one thing, my dad tells me something else. I don't know what to believe."

Cooperate when there is an emergency or crisis

Accidents and emergencies are bound to arise in family life. When they do, children need the cooperation of both parents more than ever. Animosity and blaming between parents make things harder for children. It is adding insult to injury.

Ron, the father of a five-year-old, made an appointment to see me alone. He told me there had been an accident. His son, Johnny, had fallen off the top bunk-bed onto the floor in the middle of the night and had fractured his wrist. Ron admitted to me that he had no safety bar for Johnny's bunk bed. After the accident, instead of calling Johnny's mother, Judy, Ron had called his girlfriend to come over and drive him to the hospital emergency room. An hour and a half later, after their return, he called Judy.

"Judy was furious with me for not calling her sooner. She yelled at me on the phone, and said, 'I'm his mother. You caused this accident, you idiot.' She went on and on, swearing at me."

Ron said he hung up on her, but Judy called him back a minute later. Ron tried to tell Judy that he needed to schedule a morning appointment for Johnny with an orthopedist, but he couldn't get a word in. Ron hung up on Judy again. She called him back and this time they managed to make arrangements to meet at the doctor's office later that morning.

Ron held Johnny in his arms while his girlfriend drove. Ron told me that he asked Johnny if he would like to have his father with him at the doctor's office, and when he said yes, Ron said he told his son, "Your mom likes to yell at me a lot and I don't like it. I never yell at her. If she yells at me in the doctor's office, I'll leave."

The three of them arrived simultaneously with Johnny's mother. Ron told me, "I tried to introduce my girlfriend to Judy, but Judy called her a whore and called me a bastard over

and over again in front of Johnny. I asked Judy to stop. I
pointed to Johnny, but Judy said, "I want him to know what
a bastard you are." She's trying to make me look bad in front
of my son. What does she tell Johnny about me when I'm not
there? Sometimes I feel like throwing my arms up and going
away. But I can't. I want time with my son. I think it's the
court's fault for giving custody only to one parent instead of
joint custody."

I felt great empathy for Ron, but I told him that Judy
should have been notified sooner so she could have come at
once to the emergency room, that I could see why she was so
upset.

Ron replied, "When Johnny fell down and cut his head
open and had to have stitches, she never called me at all."

I replied, "And how did that make you feel? You are
Johnny's father. Two wrongs don't make a right."

Previously, I had seen Ron and Judy together for several
sessions. I suggested that perhaps another session to discuss the
incident and to make plans for handling future emergencies or
problems might be useful. I encouraged Ron to learn from his
mistakes and to be open rather than defensive if we got together.

Ron clearly had some responsibility for the accident and
for Judy's anger, but during an emergency it is urgent that parents work together. Little Johnny's fall and injury were enough
for him to deal with at the time without the added pain of having to witness a fight between his parents.

Seek help for your child if certain symptoms persist

Many conditions are "red flags" to parents that their child
may need professional help, especially if any of the symptoms
should persist. As indicated earlier, sleep disturbances, asthma
or allergies, bedwetting, tantrums, tics or other repetitive behaviors, teeth grinding, vomiting, clinging behavior, overaggres-
sion with peers or others, daydreaming or withdrawal from
relationships, overeating or loss of appetite, diminished school

performance, delinquent behavior, self-destructive behavior, drug abuse, frequent crying or absence of emotions, difficulty talking about feelings, and siding with one parent against the other are all cause for concern.

These behaviors may spring from depression or anxiety resulting from the divorce and parental conflict, as well as the losses and changes in the child's life. Most children respond quickly to help, especially when the parents cooperate about a treatment plan. Serious consequences can result if these symptoms are ignored, or when parents refuse to cooperate.

Jennifer, age five, was an allergic and asthmatic child. Her mother, Vivian, gave her prescribed allergy medicine on a regular basis to keep her allergies in check. This seemed to lessen the frequency and severity of her asthmatic attacks. Her father, Mark, did not believe Jennifer had a problem. He did not want to be told what to do by Vivian. He refused to consult with Jennifer's doctor or to give Jennifer any medicine when she was with him. Mark also had cats, to which Jennifer was highly allergic.

One night he rushed Jennifer to the hospital emergency room. She was gasping for air. He barely made it in time to save her. After this near-tragedy, Mark and Vivian consulted with Jennifer's doctor together. Mark was instructed on how to help Jennifer and how to prevent recurrence of a severe attack.

It is unfortunate that it might take almost losing a child for some parents to realize that their child's health and well-being have to come before trying to win an argument with the other parent.

When it comes to children's well-being and potential for success, nothing can be more important for them than feeling secure, loved and cared about by both of their parents. It is my hope that the guidelines discussed in this chapter will help you create the close and loving relationship both you and your child need.

7

How Children See Divorce

The drawings in this chapter dramatically illustrate how children experience divorce. In them you will see pain and conflict expressed, as well as disbelief, confusion, anxiety, anger, frustration, guilt, sadness, hopelessness, powerlessness, despair, and love. Some children express wishes and fantasies, usually the wish that their family will be reunited, or that peace and harmony will be restored, or that there might be an end to the fighting.

The drawings were made in the waiting room outside my office by children involved in custody or visitation disputes. From hundreds of pictures I have selected these as examples of the responses children have to the stress of divorce and parental conflict.

No suggestion whatsoever was given by me to the children as to what to draw. I merely asked each of them if they wanted to draw a picture while they were waiting. If they showed an interest, I gave them crayons and a few sheets of plain 8½"x11" paper on a clipboard. I did not question them about their drawings afterward, though some children volunteered comments about what they were portraying.

Each drawing is accompanied by some factual and anecdotal information, which has been disguised to maintain confidentiality. The children's names are also fictitious.

97

The drawings on the first few pages illustrate how some children experience a divorce and subsequent custody dispute as a disaster.

Two Houses Under the Ocean

Bruce drew two houses at the bottom of the ocean. Overhead, a submarine is dropping torpedoes on the houses. He wrote the word "divorce" in jagged letters across the top.

Bruce's parents had recently separated and were constantly arguing and fighting in front of Bruce and his sister. Each parent felt threatened that he or she could lose everything, including the children. They were both extremely upset, and seemed oblivious to the pain they were causing Bruce and his sister.

It is easy for divorcing parents to lose sight of their children's feelings and needs when they are devastated and overwhelmed themselves. But, especially at this time, children experience parental arguments and conflicts as very frightening and confusing. This, coupled with a divorce, can be devastating. It shakes their inner security system to the core, leaving them weaker and less likely to succeed in whatever they undertake in life.

Drawing made by Bruce, age 9

DIVORCE IS WHAT MAKES THE
WORLD FALL APART

Bruce's sister Eileen literally drew a world cut in two. Eileen expressed her belief that divorce is what makes the world fall apart, and she views the bad part as much bigger than the good part. Her parent's arguments undoubtedly contributed heavily to making it seem that way.

During a divorce, it is not unusual for parents also to feel as if their world is falling apart. In truth, it usually does collapse on many levels, financial, emotional, and social, and in the middle of everything there are the children to raise. Children are obliged to live in the kind of world their parents create for them. Cooperation and effective communication between parents are needed to help children experience their world as a *good* and *safe* place to live.

DIVORCE is what makes the world fall apart.

bad part↓   good part↓

Drawing made by Eileen, age 10

A FAMILY STRUCK BY LIGHTNING

Jill drew bolts of lightning striking her family.

Jill had been away at summer camp when her parents separated. Coming home, she was suddenly faced with not only a divorce but also a custody battle. To her this was at least as shocking as lightning striking her family.

Children should be prepared in advance for a separation or divorce whenever possible, and arrangements should be made for frequent contact with both parents. The children should be assured that they will be well taken care of and loved by both parents even after the separation, and that the divorce will not mean total disaster for them.

Drawing made by Jill, age 11

DOOMSDAY

Dana drew what appeared to be a nuclear holocaust, with ghosts lurking everywhere. Her drawing has an eerie, dismal quality. Dana's parents had divorced many years earlier, but their bitterness remained. As a result of this bitterness, Dana had not seen her father for many years. By the time he took her mother to court for visiting rights, Dana refused to see him.

Some parents nurse resentments and bitterness from their marriage for many years after a divorce, and they allow it to ruin their children's and their own lives. Harboring resentments and grudges wastes an individual's energy and vitality. Counseling and therapy can help people free themselves from past pain, so they can enjoy life.

Children who lose contact or become estranged from one of their parents suffer deep feelings of abandonment, depression, despair, and low self-esteem.

Drawing made by Dana, age 11

The next two drawings express the confusion and disorientation that many children feel.

THE WHIRLWIND

The whirlwind of confusion depicted in this drawing parallels the current life of Ryan, who is involved in a whirlwind-like custody battle. Ryan told me that he felt caught in the middle and "that doesn't feel good."

Divorcing parents often compete and fight over their children because they feel very insecure themselves. They insist on having their children to themselves instead of sharing them. They fail to realize that neither parent can own the children, and that parents are merely given the privilege and opportunity of raising them.

Children like Ryan become anxious, insecure, and confused when their parents fight over them.

Drawing made by Ryan, age 8

FLOATING IN SPACE

Tallia expresses great insecurity in this drawing. Instead of being grounded, she draws herself as a big head with tiny legs and no body floating in space in the upper left corner of her drawing.

Tallia's mother was extremely upset after the separation and made it difficult for their father to see the children. He became frustrated and angry, and threatened to take the children from her. Tallia's mother panicked and kept the children from seeing their father and he responded by snatching them from her. During and after the divorce, Tallia and her younger brother were snatched back and forth several times, first by one parent and then the other. This is one of the most frightening and damaging experiences for a child. Disorientation and insecurity appear in Tallia's drawing.

Child-snatching is now a felony under federal law. A parent who has difficulty seeing a child may feel justified in taking that child away, but should resist the temptation for the child's sake and also in order to avoid even more serious problems in the future. It is far better for such parents to settle their problems by legal means or by mediation, which is provided in family courts and mediation centers. For a listing of such agencies, including phone numbers, see Chapter 9, *Where Help Can Be Found*.

No matter how upset parents are, they must avoid causing their children the kind of pain evident in this drawing.

Drawing made by Tallia, age 6

Some children express how torn they feel and the extreme pressure they are under during a custody dispute.

WHICH WAY SHALL I GO?

In this drawing, Mark depicts himself standing on top of a rainbow arched over two houses. Mark explained, "My parents are sliding down the rainbow into separate houses. I don't know which way to go. My legs are sticking out in both directions because I don't know which way to go."

At the time Mark made this drawing, his parents and he were still living in the family home. His drawing shows concern about having to choose between his parents once they separate. Mark's father was taking the divorce very hard. He was worried that he would lose his son the way he had lost his own father when he was five. Both parents were asking Mark to live with them.

In mediation, Mark's parents were able to agree on a joint-custody or shared-parenting plan in which Mark would spend more or less equal amounts of time with each of them. Mark's parents are to be congratulated for being willing to share him, rather than continuing to compete for him.

Drawing made by Mark, age 9

THEY'RE BOTH COMING TO HUG ME

This drawing was also made by Mark. He explained his second drawing as follows:

"My mom and dad are both coming to hug me. I don't know which one to hug first."

Mark tries hard to please both of his parents, so I gave him some simple advice: "Don't worry about which one to hug first. Just hug one and then hug the other."

Drawing made by Mark, age 9

THE PITS

In this drawing, Joseph, a gifted child, depicts himself as a stick figure hanging from a ladder suspended between two hills. He labeled the void below him "The Pits." On one hill he wrote to his dad, "I love you!" His father is telling him: "I'll give you a motorcycle." On the other hill he wrote to his mom, "I love you, too!" His mother is telling him: "Come with me, we'll have a lot of fun."

When I spoke with him, Joseph said, "My dad says my mom's not being a good mom and he wants me to come and live with him. My mom says she is a good mom, so they're going to court. I feel bad. It puts me and my sister in the middle."

Divorce tug-of-wars are extremely painful for children. Joseph's father had not been very involved in Joseph's life for many years following the divorce. After he remarried and was expecting another child, he wanted custody of Joseph and his sister "to make up for all the time he had lost." Joseph's mother was against this. She said, "I had to raise them alone, now he wants them." She wanted to punish him for his neglect. I encouraged her to let the father be more involved, even if he had not been in the past. That was what her children needed now.

In mediation, both Joseph and his sister expressed their deep desire to spend more time with their father than they had in the past. His parents settled on a shared parenting plan that allowed the children equal time with both parents. Joseph and his sister were very pleased. They got their wish, and the great pressure was off at last.

Drawing made by Joseph, age 11

FIVE DAISIES STANDING IN A ROW

Christina, Joseph's sister, also a gifted child, depicts her family as five daisies standing in a row. She colored her mother's and stepfather's petals orange, her father's and stepmother's petals purple, and her own petals half orange and half purple. She fashioned the green leaves as hearts.

She told me, "the reason my father wants me to come and live with him is because my stepmother is expecting a baby, and so he wouldn't have to pay child support if I went to live with him." She had heard her mother talking about it. "We couldn't go to my dad's house because he didn't pay child support."

She said she worries "because if I go with my mother, my dad will be sad. If I go with my dad, my mother will be sad and this problem makes me feel sad."

As part of the agreement reached by them in mediation, a statement restraining both parents from making any derogatory remarks about each other in the presence of their children was included. I received feedback more than a year later that they were keeping to their agreements—a loving gift indeed for their children.

Drawing made by Christina, age 9

Some children express strong anger, frustration, and guilt in their drawings. Frequently, the anger they portray is not their own, but comes from one or both parents.

The Prisoner

Joey drew himself as a prisoner with a ball and chain. He was involved in an exceptionally guilt-producing custody dispute. Since his parents' separation and divorce he had been living with an invalid mother who relied on Joey more and more for help and care. Joey begged his mother to let him go live with his father so he could be free to pursue sports and other activities, but Joey's mother would not give him permission to leave.

Joey's mother very much needed someone to care for her, but if Joey were burdened with her care then he would be deprived of what he needed as a young boy.

Family counseling can help in complex situations such as this. One of the goals would be to help Joey and his parents deal with Joey's anger and guilt, another would be to help Joey's mother find suitable help and care.

Drawing made by Joey, age 11

THE BIRD

During a family counseling session, Scott's mother was openly hostile toward his father in Scott's presence. I noticed a striking resemblance between the bird Scott had drawn and his mother. The resemblance had to do with her facial expression and the way she opened her mouth when she spoke angrily against his father. Scott's mother refused to restrain her anger at his father in front of Scott even when I asked her to.

Some parents are so angry with the other parent that they would like to kill him or her. Instead, they lash out with bitter words. Parents need to get their anger out, but in appropriate ways, and *not* in front of their children.

Counseling and therapy can help parents who are very angry release their hostility and regain control. Otherwise, the children get caught in the middle of the conflict and become helpless and angry themselves. Some children resent the parent who makes the angry remarks and find it increasingly difficult to be with that parent. Other children come to believe what the hostile parent says and they refuse to see the other parent. There are some children who become hostile toward both parents. No matter which way it goes, the children are the losers.

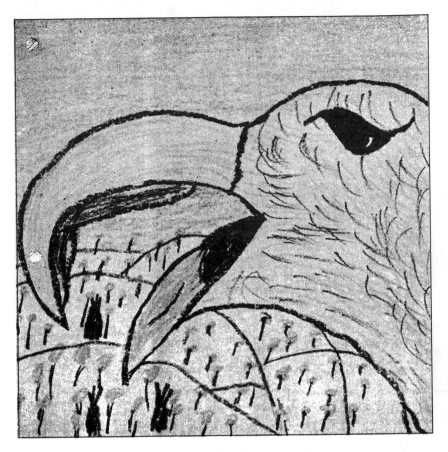

Drawing made by Scott, age 12

BLOODY MONSTER

Chris drew an angry monster and pointed out the dripping blood. His mother had run away with Chris when he was a year old and had gone into hiding. The child did not see his father and three sisters for ten years. When he was eleven, he found out how to get in touch with his father, and now he refuses to see his mother in spite of her remorse for the unfair thing she did to him.

Chris's mother had felt so trapped and unhappy in her marriage that when she had left, ten years before, all she could think of was getting out instead of seeking help. She had no money or place to go, so she left the three older children with their father, took the baby and ran. She hid for ten years, covering her tracks so her husband wouldn't find her.

During an interview, Chris said sadly, "I hate life sometimes. I should have been able to see my sisters. I get real angry at my mom and dad. Sometimes I'm mad at the whole world."

Chris may eventually learn to forgive his mother, or he may carry his unresolved anger into adulthood and allow it to ruin his life. You can imagine the feelings of abandonment his sisters will have to deal with.

I encouraged family counseling for the entire family, to help Chris and his sisters work through their pain before reaching their rebellious teenage years, when their problems would only be compounded.

Drawing made by Chris, age 11

THE FAMILY DIVIDED

Some children take sides with one parent and express this polarization in their drawings.

Tami drew a picture of herself standing with her mother. She explained that it meant that her older sister wanted to live with their father, but she and her younger sister wanted to live with their mother. Here is a family truly divided, with one child choosing to be separated from her sisters in order not to leave one of the divorcing parents.

Following separation and divorce, there is a real risk of children losing a close relationship with one or the other parent. A mother or father can help prevent this by encouraging the children to spend time with the other parent. Children need to feel that they have a home with both parents.

Drawing made by Tami, age 8

GHOSTS

Some children express fear in their drawings.

Erick drew a house surrounded by scary ghosts. During our interview, he talked about how frightened he had been when his mother's boyfriend had held him by his heels and stuck his head in the toilet while his mother stood by and did nothing. "Because I wouldn't flush it," he said.

In this situation, Erick's mother might have been so frightened and insecure herself, and so desperate for a relationship with her boyfriend, that she allowed her son to be abused by him. She is not unique, for there are insecure parents who know that their children are being sexually molested and do nothing to stop it out of fear of losing a relationship with the molester. There are other parents who abuse their own children, and they themselves may have been abused as children.

Children *must* be protected from being abused physically and emotionally. Harsh punishments and threats of punishment should be avoided. Although these punishments might appear to bring about better behavior, they can also cause serious psychological harm. Parents should look for other ways to discipline their children, and might find help in professional counseling, available in most communities through mental health agencies and family service agencies.

If, for some reason, a parent cannot provide a safe environment for his or her children, that parent should seek another living situation for them. The parent might encourage the child to live with his or her other parent until the situation improves, or seek other emergency help (see Chapter 9, *How to Find Help*.)

Drawing made by Erick, age 6

A Sad Clown

Many children express a great sadness in their drawings.

Lori had not seen her father much since the separation. After her father married a woman with two children of her own, Lori felt very left out and alone. She longed to have her father to herself sometimes, but her stepmother wouldn't hear of it.

In her drawing, Lori's depiction of herself as a sad clown was a reflection of the sadness she was experiencing. Some children experience tremendous feelings of loss, sadness, depression, rejection, and abandonment when they get less special attention from a parent who has remarried.

At the same time, Lori's stepmother was also feeling insecure and left out on the weekends that Lori came to visit. She so looked forward to being alone with her husband on weekends, especially since they both worked all week.

Two or three hours alone with a parent can often satisfy children, and it may not be necessary to exclude the stepparent for long periods. I often suggest a breakfast or early dinner in a restaurant for the mother or father and the child, or a picnic or walk or other activity during the week as an alternative to time alone on the weekend.

Drawing made by Lori, age 11

AN ARMORED ARMADILLO

Some drawings show how hard some children try not to feel anything.

Bobby sat rigidly guarded during his individual interview. He expressed little emotion when he said that he was used to his parents' arguing and fighting and he didn't care what happened.

When pain becomes extreme and continues over a long period of time, some children protect themselves with a coat of armor much like that of the armadillo in Bobby's drawing. If the conflict continues without relief, these children may remain armored and unfeeling throughout their lives, experiencing neither pain nor pleasure nor love.

It is often difficult for divorcing parents to act civil toward each other, but if they want their children to grow into loving, caring, feeling people, they *must* create a tolerable situation for them when they are young.

Drawing made by Bobby, age 7

THE GOOD TIMES AND THE BUMMERS

Linda's parents had been separated several months. Both her younger sister and she said they did not want to live with either parent because of the terrible arguments and fights their parents were having over money. They asked to be able to live with a cousin for a while until their parents calmed down and were able to settle their financial squabbles. After Linda made this drawing, I asked whether her life was a good time or a bummer. She replied sadly, "Mostly bummers."

Many parents go through a very stormy period before and after separation and during that period they find it difficult to control their behavior. The two faces drawn by Linda clearly indicate the emotional ups and downs she has been through. This could have been avoided if her parents had kept their quarrels private.

Drawing made by Linda, age 12

THIS IS HOW I FEEL AND THIS IS
WHAT IS HAPPENING

Some children describe what is happening in their lives and what they want to happen.

Amy drew a picture of herself standing in a rainstorm with a big frown on her face. Her wish, she told me, was that her parents would stop fighting. When her mother and father reached an agreement, Amy was ecstatic. "I got my wish," she said joyously.

Unfortunately, this was not the end of her parents' conflicts. Two years later Amy made a second drawing which showed her parents arguing over Amy. Though it was done in cartoon fashion, it was not funny. Amy stated clearly that she did not want her parents to argue when her mother came to pick her up.

Parents who remain connected or bonded in a negative way after a divorce continue to go round and round, never ending their conflict or freeing themselves to live happily. It is tormenting for a child when these battles continue year after year. Such parents owe it to themselves and to their children to seek individual help or postdivorce counseling (see Chapter 9).

Drawings made by Amy, age 8,
and Amy, age 10

Ruler of the Mountain

Some children express their feelings of powerlessness.

Ricky is yet another child who was snatched back and forth. First his mother took him and he did not see his father for years. Then he was snatched by his father, and his mother vanished from his life. He was too young and powerless to do anything about this.

In his drawing, Ricky reveals his deep wish to be *powerful*. He depicts himself as "ruler of the highest mountain," an extremely powerful being indeed. Some children like Ricky who feel powerless in their youth never shed this feeling of impotence as they grow into adulthood.

Violence between parents, threats of violence and feelings of extreme insecurity can lead some parents into taking off with the children. This, of course, leads to retaliation by the other parent, and the children get caught in the middle.

Parents who are feeling threatened can find help without putting their children through the pain of being fugitives. Only parents can give children the *power of security* that they long for.

Drawing made by Ricky, age 12

DADDY, LOOK, A PUPPY

Some drawings show the child's secret desire for contact with a parent.

Tammy told me that she did not want to see her father because he was not paying child support and had left her mother for another woman. Tammy's choice of words, her tone of voice and her facial expressions were exactly like her mother's. In spite of Tammy's angry words, however, in her drawing she depicted herself as having a friendly interaction with her father, telling him, "Daddy, look, a puppy." Her father's response to her is, "We'll name it Dusty."

Children like Tammy long for a close relationship with both of their parents, but are forced to take sides with an angry, hostile parent because otherwise they are afraid they will lose that parent's love.

Tammy's mother meant Tammy no harm. She felt so betrayed by and bitter toward Tammy's father that all she thought about was how she could hurt him back for all the pain he had caused her. She was not thinking about Tammy's need to have a father. I pointed out the harm she was causing Tammy and how her behavior could destroy Tammy's chances for a happy life.

Fortunately, she believed me. She agreed that Tammy could begin spending weekends with her father and that she would take Tammy for some family counseling sessions. Tammy looked amazed and relieved when she found out that she could see her father on weekends. I give her mother a lot of credit for being willing to listen and change her attitude and behavior. It takes a big person to admit he or she is wrong.

Drawing made by Tammy, age 8

When My Daddy Was Living Here

Some children remember the past in their drawings.

Sara remembers a time when her parents were still living together. In her drawing, she tells the story of how her sister poured Cheerios all over the floor when her daddy was living with them.

Children tend to hold on to memories of how life was before the divorce. Since children do not understand adult problems, some blame themselves or their siblings for the breakup. *Children should be told that they did not cause the divorce.* They should be given a simple explanation for what happened that blames neither parent. In reality both parents are responsible, in some way, for the problems that led to the divorce.

It takes a lot of courage for parents to be honest and to acknowledge their own part in what has happened in their lives. It is so much easier to blame it all on the other parent, even though it is so much harder on their children.

my sister poured cheerios all over the floor when my dady was living here.

Cheerios

Drawing made by Sara, age 10

FAMILY WITH BALLOONS

Some children express fantasies in their drawings that deny the reality of the divorce.

Ellie's parents had separated recently. They told me that Ellie had been very upset by the separation. In her drawing she depicted all of her family standing in a row, with her mother next to her father, and her brother and she holding balloons, just as if her family were out on a joyous outing and the separation had never happened.

Disbelief or denial is the first stage in the long grieving process. It can take children and parents two to three years to recover and heal from a divorce. Denial is Ellie's defense against facing and feeling the pain of the divorce. She needs reassurance from both parents that she will be loved and taken care of, even though they live apart. As the grieving process continues, Ellie is likely to experience anger, anxiety, and sadness, and eventually come to accept the divorce as a reality. Then she can heal and grow.

Drawing made by Ellie, age 9

THE COZY COTTAGE

The cozy cottage drawn by Diana symbolizes the kind of home that most children long for. When parents are willing to cooperate following separation and divorce, children are able to experience having not one but *two* cozy nests, one with Dad and one with Mom.

Shared parenting arrangements give children the security of having two involved parents in their lives. There are many kinds of shared parenting or joint-custody plans from which to choose. Children can spend equal amounts of time in both homes, or more time during the week with one parent and more weekend and vacation time with the other parent (see Chapter 4).

Drawing made by Diana, age 9

MY AUNT'S HOUSE

Tina drew a picture of herself at her aunt's house. Later, during her interview alone with me, she told me of her wish to live with her aunt: "She has a pretty house and no children. She's like a mother and she takes me places."

Since her parents' separation, Tina had been living with her father. She had not seen her mother for a year, and did not want to see her because she drank too much. Tina was afraid that her mother would take her away and not bring her back. She appeared to be searching for a "good" mother, one who would not leave her, one who did not drink or make her feel fearful.

Children need *two* parents they can trust and feel safe with. Grandparents, stepparents, aunts, uncles, and others are also important, but they do not make up for a close relationship with parents.

Parents who have a drug addiction or a drinking problem owe it to themselves and their children to seek help. The other parent should make every effort to help the child, by keeping in close contact or re-establishing contact if he or she was estranged. Even sporadic visits have been found to be better for a child than no visits at all. Counseling can be helpful when children do not want to see a parent.

Drawing made by Tina, age 9

Many children express tremendous love in their drawings, but for some, the love is very sad.

THE SAD KNIGHT

Shawn drew a knight with a sad dog's face and a man's body, legs, and feet. The knight is carrying a bow and arrow. There is a big teardrop falling from each of the sad knight's eyes, and overhead, a broken heart.

Shawn's parents were competing for Shawn's love, and each asked him to choose where he wanted to live. Shawn did not want to hurt either his mother or his father. He wished he could live with both his parents.

Children should not be asked where they want to live. This puts them in a no-win situation. Parents should never put this kind of pressure on their children, even when they feel lonely and insecure themselves. It is the responsibility of both parents to create a new life for themselves after divorce, without drawing on their young children for support. For parents who feel lost there is counseling or therapy, and many fine support groups (see Chapter 9).

Drawing made by Shawn, age 7

A HEART BIGGER THAN A HOUSE

Mia expressed tremendous love for her mother and father in her drawing. She told me sadly that her parents argued over the telephone and when her father came to pick her up. "It makes me feel bad. I wish they would stop."

Regarding the separation, Mia said, "My daddy left and I didn't see him go. I don't get to see him very much. I'm glad my dad will be taking me to ballet now. I'll get to see him more."

During a mediation session a few hours earlier, Mia's parents had reached an agreement to increase her father's time with Mia. At one point during the session, Mia's mother had suddenly become very angry with me when I talked about the child's need to have a close relationship with both parents. She said furiously, "He has gone out of his way to be disruptive. You don't understand how terrible he is. Why do you think it's important for Mia to see her father more?" Then she broke down and sobbed, "I suppose you would have thought it was important for me to see my father. He raped me from three to seven years old. He was in jail for years. He also raped his stepchildren."

After she calmed down, I helped her realize that Mia's father was not like her own father. She reconsidered and agreed that Mia could see her father more often.

Because Mia's mother had been abused as a child, she was still living in the past and not seeing that her daughter needed a close relationship with her own father, who was *not* abusing Mia. Mia's mother needed someone to help her sort out her past pain and fears from the present, and to help her focus on Mia's need to have a father.

Drawing made by Mia, age 6

A HEART IS BEAUTIFUL

Lisa told me that her parents fought a lot but that the fighting would stop once the divorce was final. Unfortunately, given the situation, that was unlikely to happen. Her father would not settle for less than equal time with his children, and her mother was deeply opposed to this. Lisa continued, "Daddy says he loves my mom, but my mom says he lies. I can't pick sides, but she doesn't have to hate him. If I was getting a divorce, I wouldn't hate. I wouldn't hang up."

When asked about how their fighting made her feel, she replied, "I don't feel good. They're grown up but they act like babies. I don't like the way they're acting. I get stuck in the middle. That's not fair to me. They can't talk, so my mom asks me to tell my dad things. I can't wait until the divorce is over. If that's what will make them happy, then I'll be happy. I can't wait for that day."

I didn't have the heart to tell Lisa that some parents continue fighting forever. It is up to parents to end the conflict. Once the marriage is over, it does *no one* any good to keep rehashing the past. To shift gears from being marriage partners to being parent partners requires the parents focusing on the present (not on the past) and on the children's needs and how best to meet those needs. Parents do not have to like each other to be parent partners. They just have to love their children.

Drawing made by Lisa, age 10

Peace and Harmony

Brigette drew a peaceful scene and wrote, "Peace and Harmony." During her interview with me, she told me how frightened she was when her parents used to fight. "I was in my room crying. They love each other but they don't want to show it."

The peace and harmony that Brigette is pleading for *is possible to achieve*. No matter how difficult and terrible things have been in the past, parents still have the power to create a better, more peaceful situation for themselves and for their children.

Drawing made by Brigette, age 9

SYMMETRY

Perfect symmetry was drawn by Dayton, a sensitive boy involved in a vicious custody battle, indicating his need for an orderly, harmonious life.

One way that parents can help restore order and symmetry in their own lives, and in their children's lives, is by agreeing on a suitable parenting plan that can meet their children's needs *as soon as possible*. There are a great many different plans to choose from (see Chapter 4).

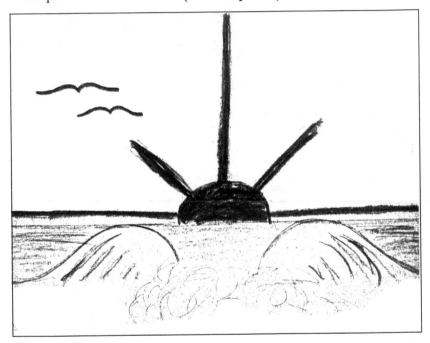

Drawing made by Dayton, age 12

Many children express their deep need and longing for peace and harmony in their lives—an end to parental conflict.

PEACE FROG

Debbie drew a big green frog and labeled it "Peace Frog." Debbie's mother had been accusing Debbie's father of not caring about the children; Debbie's father had been telling Debbie that her mother was crazy, and Debbie kept longing for peace.

Debbie's parents had not yet learned how to be parent partners. They were still stuck in the past, hurting, accusing, blaming, and shaming each other. When parents cannot let the past go, they can't really enjoy the present or future. One good reason for closing the door on the past is that a brighter, more peaceful present and future are then possible. It also allows their children to experience love and harmony in their lives, and gives them a model for resolving conflict.

Drawing made by Debbie, age 14

HAVE A RAINBOW DAY

Betty wishes everyone a "rainbow day," although the raindrops are still falling in her life. This drawing was Betty's way of expressing her deep wish for the "storm" in her family to pass over, and for peace and normalcy to prevail. A rainbow symbolizes hope, an end to the storm, a return of sunlight and joy, and the dawning of a new and brighter day.

It is often very difficult for divorcing parents to leave the pain from the marriage behind. There is a strong desire to blame the other parent for everything that happened and to punish the other parent for causing them pain. This perpetuates the storm and in the end, brings no satisfaction for anyone. A healing affirmation that parents might say to themselves is the following: "My children are counting on me. What happened in the past is over. I will learn from my experiences, accept my losses, and create a new beginning for myself and my children."

Drawing made by Betty, age 10

The Message Conveyed by the Drawings

These poignant drawings reveal the true depth of these children's feelings, and tell how much children are in touch with the main issues and how they try to handle and integrate their experiences.

Children's art, as well as original stories, fantasies, dreams and play, can be therapeutic tools for helping children, and an excellent medium for discovering the inner world of the child. Here I have purposely done little psychological interpretation of these drawings. I saw no need to do so since each drawing is self-explanatory, and tells its own story.

The message of these drawings is very clear. These children and untold numbers like them are involved in intolerable situations which can only lead to frustration and unhappiness from generation to generation. Many children are in a no-win situation that keeps them in a state of torment throughout their entire childhood. To make matters worse, the quality of their lives does not improve in adulthood, either because of the many unhappy memories and experiences that they carry with them from their childhood.

The positive side to all of this is that parents can learn to get along after divorce and that children are very resilient and can heal rather quickly if they are given half a chance. It is my hope that these drawings will inspire parents to work together cooperatively so that their children can feel good about their lives and the chain of unhappiness can be broken forever.

8

Handling Difficult Situations

The questions and answers below give parents information and suggestions on how to handle a wide variety of delicate and difficult situations that affect many divorcing or divorced parents and their children (See *References*, 3.) They are reproduced from a column called "For Better or Worse" that I wrote for three years for the Santa Monica *Independent Journal*. All the situations are real, only the names have been changed.

My responses to these questions are a first step toward improving a difficult situation; they are not meant to be cure-alls, and professional help should be considered to meet the wider demands of any situation.

One Parent Has Difficulty Accepting the Divorce

Dear Florence:

My wife is divorcing me. We have two young kids. We separated eight months ago and I can't stand it. I don't want the divorce. I don't believe in breaking up the family. I still love my wife, but she won't let me come into my own house. I'm all broken up about it. Once, when I went there to kiss the kids, I got so upset I almost choked her, and I threatened to take the kids away from her. A divorce is going to hurt our kids. Since she wants the divorce, why should she get them? Why doesn't she just go away and leave us alone? If she ends-up getting the kids, I'm going to go away and never see her or the kids again.

Signed

P———.

Dear P:

You are in great pain and you are not thinking clearly right now. It is not unusual for people who are going through a divorce to feel as if they are going crazy. At a time like this, some people do and say terrible things. Your indication that either you will go away and never see the children again or your wife should leave you and the kids alone shows that you are not thinking of the children. The children need *both* of you. When two people with children divorce each other, they don't stop being parents. Your children need a lot of contact with each of you. If they should lose either of you, it would break their hearts. I suggest you and she work out a plan that allows both of you to spend a lot of time with the children. If you're too upset to work together, then seek counseling for yourself until you feel better and are thinking more clearly. Above all, avoid physical violence or making threats.

Regarding the divorce, if her mind is truly made up to divorce you, there is nothing you can do except learn from your mistakes and cooperate in raising the children. It would be helpful if you could accept some responsibility for causing the divorce. This will enable you to become a stronger person. You and she both created your relationship the way it was, for better or worse.

I suggest that you not pressure her about coming back to you, or give her a hard time about the divorce. If there is a chance for the two of you, that would only ruin it. As painful as this time is for you, I would like to see you use this crisis as a turning point in your life from which to grow and gain in self-awareness, self-respect, and self-control.

Custody Disputes Are Tied to
Who Gets the House

Dear Florence:

My wife and I are getting a divorce. We have two children, and I want joint custody, but my wife won't agree to it. She thinks if she gets custody she'll get to stay in the house. I think the house should be sold, because then we will both have money to each make a home for our children. I want my kids to live half the time with me. They need me, too. I'm really frustrated. She's only thinking of herself.

Signed

M——.

Dear M:

It is unfortunate that some parents let financial issues get in the way of settling child-custody arrangements. Getting custody of the children does not necessarily mean that a parent will get the house. Children are *not* possessions. They do not automatically go with the house. It is better for children when parents keep the financial issues separate and settle on a parenting arrangement that will best meet their children's needs.

You might try putting your financial proposal in writing and sending it to your children's mother for consideration. It is not unusual for divorcing parents to mistrust each other. Your ideas and solutions may seem very fair to you, but not at all fair to her. Be willing to compromise a little to reach an agreement.

It is also not unusual for parents to become suspicious, anxious, and even panicky about the many losses that occur as a result of a divorce. The stresses can become overwhelming.

One option open to parents who cannot agree on financial issues is divorce mediation. You might wish to propose this to her for consideration. In the event that no agreement is reached, you can each hire an attorney to handle your financial settlement. Perhaps with your attorneys' help, you and she will be able to reach a stipulated settlement between yourselves. As a last resort a judge can decide. No matter which way it goes, neither one of you is apt to feel that the financial settlement was fair.

Sometimes it can take years for financial issues to be settled. In the meantime, *it is essential that parents cooperate regarding their children*. Children cannot be put on "hold" until the details of a financial settlement are decided. They deserve and need a livable situation in the meantime.

A Father Is Refused Visitation Because He Can't Pay Child Support

Dear Florence:

I'm divorced and I have a three-year-old son who lives with my former wife. I'm not working now and I can't pay child support, so she won't let me see my son. I haven't seen him for four months, and I want to see him for Christmas. Is there anything I can do?

Signed

C———.

Dear C:

You have the right to see your son and he has the right to see you. He needs you all year round, not just on Christmas. Access to your son should not be denied because you are not paying child support. No matter how frustrated your son's mother feels, she does not have the legal or moral right to keep your son from seeing you. This only hurts your son more. You might call on a fathers' rights group, a legal clinic, or a law school where you can obtain some free legal advice in your area.

At the same time, your son's mother is right. You should be paying child support and taking some responsibility for your son's care. It will make your son's life much easier if this cause of resentment is resolved. Perhaps the Department of Human Resources can help you find a job. Also check ads in local newspapers regularly.

This Christmas you may be down and out, but you can create a better Christmas for yourself next year and from now on, if you stop seeing yourself as a victim. We all wish there was a Santa Claus who could bring us the solution to our problems. Unfortunately, there is not. It is all up to you. But by solving these problems yourself you will become stronger.

A Mother Wants to Know How to Help Her Child Accept the Divorce

Dear Florence:

My husband and I are planning to divorce. Our marriage has been bad for a long time. We've had marriage counseling but nothing has helped. Now I'm in love with another man and I plan to marry him. The big problem is our eight-year-old daughter, Tammy. She begs me to tell her daddy I love him and not to see the other man. Tammy is very close to her father. He tells her he doesn't like my friend, so Tammy is afraid to like him. What can I do to help Tammy accept the divorce?

Signed

N——.

Dear N:

It is not unusual for children to be upset by a divorce. Most children want their parents to love each other and stay together. Children go through various stages of mourning much as adults do, from disbelief to bargaining to anger to sadness and depression, and eventually to acceptance of the divorce.

One way you can help Tammy is by letting her express her sadness to you. Let her know that you and her father will *not* be living together anymore and explain to her that she is *not* going to lose you or her father, that both you and her father will continue to take care of her, and that she can love you and her father and many other good people in her life.

You might wish to give Tammy some simple explanation or reason for the divorce without blaming anyone, such as "Daddy and I have problems and we can't work it out," or "Daddy and I aren't happy together." She does not have to hear all the details. The main thing that children want to hear is that they will still be loved and cared for.

Tammy's father must be feeling very threatened at present. I suggest you let him know as soon as possible that you want to cooperate with him about Tammy, that you know he's a good father, and that you are willing to arrange a meeting to discuss a parenting plan that will allow both of you to spend a lot of time with your child.

I also suggest that you ask your friend to be patient with Tammy and let her warm up to him slowly and gradually, without trying to force her to like him "right now." By this time next year all of you should be doing much better. If not, seek help.

A Parent Is Concerned About the Way a Child Is Being Treated by the Other Parent

Dear Florence:

My twelve-year-old daughter comes back after visiting her dad and complains to me about him. Last time she said he called her stupid and made her feel bad. She says she doesn't want to go with him anymore. I think he is too hard on her. He thinks I'm too easy. What can I do? I don't want to force her to go.

Signed

E——.

Dear E:

If her father is willing to discuss the problem with you, let him know in a nonthreatening manner that your daughter is upset and her feelings are hurt. If he won't discuss it with you, then back off, and when she complains to you about her father and says she doesn't want to see him, listen to what she has to say, then encourage her to talk to her father about it. It is best if you do not interfere in their relationship. Let them work it out between the two of them. In that way her father is less likely to blame you for this problem. He will have to deal with his daughter directly.

She may also be complaining about you to her father. Some children manipulate both parents and tell each one what they think he or she wants to hear. This usually happens in situations where parents do not get along and are not cooperating with each other. Children are less likely to try this form of manipulation if parents work together cooperatively.

Parents differ widely in the way they handle their children; some are very strict, others highly permissive. This can be true of parents who remain together, but it is easy for one divorcing parent to use these differences as an excuse to keep the children away from the other parent.

I am strongly against calling children stupid, because it can be harmful to a child's self-image, but I caution you about talking to your daughter against her father, or pointing out his faults to her. This could make the problem between them even worse and harm your daughter in the end.

If this situation doesn't improve soon I suggest you try family counseling. Invite the other parent to participate also, so your daughter and her father can work this out together.

A Father Thinks It Is Better
Not to See His Child

Dear Florence:

Since my wife and I went to court in April, I've been seeing my four-and-a-half-year-old daughter Robin on alternate weekends. When it's time to drop her off after the weekend, she cries and hangs on to me pathetically. She tells me she doesn't want to leave me, and it breaks me up. Wouldn't it be easier on her if I didn't see her at all?

Signed

S———.

Dear S:

No, it would be harder on her if you stopped seeing her. I sense your pain at seeing your little girl become so upset, but she needs to keep seeing you regularly. She is just having a difficult time seeing you so infrequently and when she does see you, it is hard for her to give you up. Most little girls are very attached to their daddies. She will probably get used to the schedule eventually, but perhaps you could arrange with her mother to see Robin more often—for example, one additional evening each week for dinner from 5:30 to 7:30, or overnight. Also, telephone her at least once a week to say hello. The main thing is for you to keep seeing her regularly. If you stop seeing her, she will be absolutely brokenhearted and will probably never get over the hurt.

There Are Constant Hassles Between Parents

Dear Florence:

I'm very frustrated. My wife and I separated last summer. Ever since then we have been having constant hassles over the children. I say one thing and she says the opposite. Our kids are being torn apart. She's so changeable. I never know what to expect. When she's feeling all right, I get to see my kids; when she's angry or upset, I don't. We can't talk without arguing, and my kids overhear us. When I go to pick up the kids they aren't ready, and sometimes when I return them she's not there. I have had to wait with them in the car for two hours until she came home. I know it's wrong, but when I get mad at her I mail the child support check to her a week late to get even. I don't like to play that game, but I get so mad. I just wish she'd be more considerate about my feelings.

It's an awful mess. I feel sorry for my kids. They are really bright, but now they are not doing well in school. Do you have any suggestions?

Signed

G——.

Dear G:

Your children need relief from these constant hassles. I am glad that you are motivated to help. You and their mother need to learn how to work together, for children can recover from a divorce but not when they are being pulled back and forth in this way.

Your separation is fairly recent. It takes time for raw emotions to heal, and your children's mother will probably calm down and become more reasonable and predictable to deal with. In the meantime, keep as calm as possible yourself. You do have the right to see your children, and it may become necessary for you to obtain legal assistance in order to secure your rights if she continues to be uncooperative. Once the court has ordered specific times for you to see your children, she will have to comply or she can be held in contempt of court.

Regarding your sending the child support payment to her late: Admittedly, it is her responsibility to see that your children are ready on time for you to pick them up, and to be home to receive them when it's time for you to drop them off again. However, it is also your responsibility to keep your agreements, including mailing the child support money on time. Two wrongs don't make a right. Mailing the child support payment late makes things worse, and I'm sure she finds ways of getting even. The children sense what is going on between you two and they probably feel very upset and uneasy about it.

Even if you think she started the whole thing and is completely to blame, my suggestion for improving the situation is that you apologize to her for mailing the child support checks late in the past, and tell her it won't happen again. If you begin with an apology, she may be less defensive, more willing to acknowledge her own mistakes, and more cooperative in the future.

If she continues to be out when you return the children, I suggest you wait thirty minutes, and then write her a note telling her how long you waited and that you have taken the children home with you. Say nothing more. It will then be her responsibility to call and come to pick up the children herself. Don't make a scene about this when she calls or comes. Stay calm and give her the children. This will either discourage her from being late or, if not, at least give you extra time with your children.

If your children are doing poorly in school, I suggest you ask the school counselor for a referral for postdivorce family counseling and invite their mother to participate. If she refuses, ask the family counselor to get in touch with her. Maybe then she will accept.

It takes two of you to have these constant arguments, and it sounds like there is a power struggle going on. If either of you would back off once in a while, it might defuse the situation. Without so much conflict your children will probably be very relieved and begin doing better in school, although they may still need some tutoring to help them catch up.

A Parent Believes One Visit a Month Is Enough for a Child

Dear Florence:

I have a two-and-a-half-year-old son, Jason. His father left us just after Jason was born. I hadn't even recuperated from the delivery. He's been seeing Jason about once a month in my home, but now he is demanding to see Jason more often. I don't want Jason going back and forth. Once a month is enough. Now Jason feels secure. He knows who his mother is.

Signed

M——.

Dear M:

It's good that Jason knows who his mother is. Seeing his father more often will not confuse Jason about his relationship with you. But Jason also needs to know who his father is. I do not believe that once a month is often enough for a young child to see a parent. I suggest a minimum of once a week or even more often, if possible, especially while Jason is so young. Let his father spend the time with Jason outside your home. It is extremely uncomfortable for one parent to visit in the other parent's home, and Jason must sense the tension between you two.

Jason's father left you at a very difficult time, when you were very dependent on him because of your weakened physical condition. You probably felt totally abandoned by him, almost like a child. But you must not let the pain and hurt you felt then be transmitted to your son now. He needs his father, and if he does not see his father more often, Jason, too, is likely to feel abandoned by him, and this could lead to serious problems for your son later on. If you are not able to let go of your hurt and anger toward Jason's father, seek counseling help for yourself.

I suggest you encourage Jason's father to participate more in his son's life, so Jason can have a successful relationship with both of you. Also, allow him to share some responsibility for caring for Jason instead of trying to carry the entire responsibility yourself. Both you and Jason will benefit.

A Father Is Gay

Dear Florence:

A year ago my husband told me he is gay. I was shocked. I've known him since high school. We've been married for five years. I never imagined he was gay. He hid it from me entirely, and I'm very angry that he deceived me, for I would not have had a child with him if I had known. He says he loves me and he wants to stay married, but since he has refused to give up his homosexual activities, I have asked him to leave. He wants to see our three-year-old son a lot, but I told him I don't want our son around his gay friends or left alone with them. I'm afraid my son will be harmed, and I'm worried he might become gay too. My husband has promised to be discreet when our son is with him, but I don't trust him. Should I prevent him from seeing his son?

Signed

B——.

Dear B:

Your son needs a relationship with his father, even if the father is gay. As long as he has promised to be discreet when your son is with him, it would be wise to give your husband the benefit of the doubt. I do not suggest that you keep your son from his father or try to control which friends his father sees when your son is with him. It is unlikely your husband will "push" his homosexuality on his son or allow his son to be molested by other men.

Your relationship with your son will also have a strong influence on his sexual preferences when he is older. When little boys have a close and loving relationship with their mothers, they tend to transfer that love to another woman and become heterosexual. Likewise, little girls transfer their love from father to another man later on. In other words, your son won't become gay just because his father is gay. The less worry, attention and energy you put on it, the less of an issue this will be for your son, and the less chance he will have of becoming gay. So you might as well relax about it and be the best mom you can be.

A Mother Feels Powerless

Dear Florence:

I left my husband about a year and a half ago. After I left

him, he often harassed me and threatened me and my boy-friend. Once he took our two children, three and four years old, away for two days. I was such a wreck that I saw a psychiatrist; I was ready to put myself away. He had all the money, so he kept the house and I lived in a little hovel, letting the children stay with him. Since I agreed to this I've been seeing them only one day a week and every other weekend.

I want to spend more time with my children and they want to see more of me. I want joint custody, so that the children can live with me one week and with their father one week. He says he'll let me have them for two weeks and then he'll have them for two weeks if I pay for half of their nursery school tuition and if I drive them 120 miles back and forth to school every day. I have no job and no money. He won't help me share the driving or change their school so they will be closer to me. He holds all the cards. When we went through the divorce, I was so intimidated by him and so upset, I gave him everything. I'm tired of being poor and I can't afford a lawyer to take him back to court. What can I do?

Signed

L———.

Dear L:

Many people going through a divorce feel as if they're going crazy and can't cope with all the stress. As a result, many parents get off to a bad start in planning for themselves and for their children. If possible, I suggest that you move closer to your children's father so they won't have to be transported so far every day. That is a lot of driving daily with young children, and it may be a hardship for them and for you. A two-week period is too long a stretch for young children not to see you or their father, but if you decide on that plan the children could spend the weekend in the middle of that two-week period with the other parent.

In case you can't move closer together, another plan you might wish to consider is keeping to the schedule you have now during the school year, and having the children spend the entire summer vacation and more time during winter and spring vacations with you. During the summer, the children could spend one day during the week and alternate weekends with their father.

Whichever plan you agree upon, the main thing is that the children have the chance to spend time with both of you. Their security will come from feeling that both of you love them and take care of them. You can't go back and do the financial settlement over again. It is too bad you didn't get good legal advice at the time.

It is important for your own well-being that you stop seeing yourself as a victim, and begin thinking of yourself as a worthwhile person who has the power to create a good life for yourself and your children.

There are a number of agencies that might be able to offer you assistance. Call the Department of Public Social Services in your area and ask what help you can qualify for. Perhaps you can get food stamps and Medicaid, since you plan to have the children live with you half the time. The Department of Human Resources in your area may be able to help you find work, and may also have job training programs available. Perhaps you can obtain free advice at a legal clinic or law school in your area regarding child-custody issues and child support. Last but not least, *get some counseling for yourself.* There are family counseling agencies or mental health agencies that provide help for little or no money. Inquire around until you find one that will take you. Begin working with a counselor until you get on your feet and feel really good about yourself and your life. As long as you continue to see yourself as your former husband's victim and continue to blame him for all your problems, nothing good can happen for you or your children.

(Many of the services mentioned in this letter are discussed in detail in Chapter 9, *Where to Find Help.* It includes information on emergency, psychological and legal services for families; parent support groups; county conciliation courts; and family court mediation services.)

A Father Is a Stranger to His Young Child

Dear Florence:

My husband and I separated when our daughter, Tina, was six months old. He didn't come around or even call for three months. When he finally did call and wanted to see Tina, I was so angry I refused to let him see her. Now Tina is almost a year old and she doesn't know her father. He wants to pick up my baby twice a week and take her to his place, but how can I give Tina to a total stranger?

Signed

Y——.

Dear Y:

It is extremely important that a relationship be reestablished between Tina and her father. This should be done as soon as possible and as gradually as necessary, so as not to traumatize her. I suggest for the first few weeks that Tina's father spend a few hours with Tina once or twice a week in your home, with either you present or a neutral person with whom Tina is familiar. You or your substitute should take a back seat and allow Tina's father to play with her and take care of her. After Tina is familiar with her father, he could begin to take her out for a few hours to his home, or to a nearby park once or twice a week for several weeks. Within two months Tina should be ready to spend at least one entire day each week with her father. One month or so after that, overnights could begin.

At first it may be difficult for you to let her go, especially since mothers of infants feel extremely protective and attached to their new babies. After the first few times it should become easier for you.

I suggest you be as cordial and cooperative as you can. You and Tina's father are going to have a long association of being parents together. The way you and he get along together will determine whether your child's life is peaceful or painful. I urge you to cooperate in making this possible for her. Isn't she worth all the trouble you will have to go through to do this?

One Parent Plans to Move Away
with the Children

Dear Florence:

My husband is divorcing me, and I plan to take our two small children back to Nevada, where my parents live. My husband is angry because I am moving away and threatens to fight for custody of the children. Is there any way we can avoid an ugly custody battle?

Signed

T———.

Dear T:

This is a very difficult situation, especially since your children are so young. Young children need a mother and a father they can relate to and touch.

It is extremely important that their father remain involved in their lives. If you must move away, try to work out a parenting plan before you leave. This could help you avoid a custody battle. If the children live with you during the school year, they could spend the summer and other school vacations with their father. You and he might wish to consider alternating this pattern every few years or so, with telephone conversations and correspondence between visits.

I suggest you reassure your children's father that you intend to cooperate with him about arranging for him to see the children. He must be feeling extremely threatened about losing them. If the two of you are unable to reach an agreement, you may wish to try divorce mediation. As a last resort, a judge may have to decide this matter.

One Parent Is Living with Another
Man or Woman

Dear Florence:

My husband left us for another woman. Now he wants to

see my son and he wants Robert to attend his wedding. I refuse to let Robert go there as long as his father is living with that woman, and Robert doesn't want to go to the wedding because he knows how much I've been hurt. I surely don't want Robert turning out like his father. Am I doing the right thing?

Signed

F——.

Dear F:

Even though you are still very angry because your son's father left you for another woman, it is important for Robert to see his father. He left you, not Robert, and no matter what you think of your former husband, Robert still has the right to know him. I do not believe that one parent has the right to exclude the other parent because that parent is living with another woman (or man).

Your attitude has caused Robert to side with you and to feel sorry for you. He feels that he must protect you. If you want him to be happy, free him by encouraging him *not* to take sides. In spite of how hurt you feel, I believe it is important that Robert attend his father's wedding. Give him your permission and encouragement. You might tell him something like this: "No matter what has happened between your father and me, he is still your father and he wants you to attend his wedding. I would want you to attend my wedding, if I were getting married again."

The more you resist allowing Robert to know his father, the more he will want to. Your effort to keep Robert away from his father may eventually backfire. I urge you not to say anything derogatory to Robert about his father, as this would only hurt your son.

Regarding your concern that Robert might turn out to be like his father, Robert will have his own experience of you and of his father, and he will choose to be the kind of a man he wishes to be. What you can do is be the best parent *you* can and make a good life for Robert and yourself when he is with you. That is all any parent can do.

One Parent Feels Manipulated by
the Other Parent

Dear Florence:

My husband and I are getting a divorce after a terrible twelve-and-a-half-year marriage. He was a dreadful husband, interested only in his career. Since we separated two months ago, he's been trying to manipulate me through the children. He sees them on Tuesday and Thursday evening, for dinner and every weekend except one per month. Sometimes my children, who are five and eight years old, have their own activities. He's willing to make changes so they can go, as long as I make up that time to him! For example, if my eight-year-old has some activity to go to on Tuesday evening, his father wants me to let him see the children on Wednesday evening instead; or if they are sick he expects me to give him my time with them. What rights do I have? I want to be able to plan things, too. I know I'm being stubborn, but I'm not married to him anymore and I'm not going to make any changes to suit him.

Signed

A——.

Dear A:

The way I see this situation is that all of you have rights. Your children have the right to be with you, to be with their father, and to have interests, relationships, and activities of their own. Their father has the right to have time with the children, and this is in your children's best interests also. It is fortunate that he is willing to switch evenings so your children can attend their activities on his evening. If he were willing, he could spend that evening or weekend with the children and take them for their activities himself. You also have a right to be with the children, but not to plan activities during his time or to take his time away from him.

It is important for parents to be flexible and willing to make occasional changes to accommodate the children so they can continue their activities. Juggling schedules can be frustrating even when parents live together, and it becomes more complicated after divorce. Parents can get extremely protective of their time with the children, because they are frightened of losing them and frightened of being dominated or manipulated by the other parent. As difficult as your situation may seem at times, it would be far worse for the children if their father did not want to see them.

You and he have recently separated, and it will probably take a while for both of you to feel less angry and threatened. Even if you do not want to make any changes to accommodate your children's father, I believe some flexibility is important, especially for special occasions or unusual circumstances; otherwise your children will be the losers. Getting even with him for being a "terrible" husband during the marriage by being totally rigid about the schedule will end by hurting your children most of all. On the other hand, you don't have to allow yourself to become a martyr or be constantly inconvenienced by him either.

In general, it sounds like your children have a good situation. I commend you both for thinking about your children's needs and I encourage you to cooperate as much as possible, so that things can go smoothly for your children.

A Parent Takes a Child Away

Dear Florence:
I'm having a terrible time. My former husband took our four-year-old son Brian to Hawaii and he won't return him to me. Hawaii is where we lived before I left my husband, but after we separated I took Brian and moved to California. Now he's threatening that if I don't move back there, he'll obtain custody of Brian and I'll never be able to see him again. What can I do?

Signed

B——.

Dear B:

I suggest you seek legal advice as soon as possible. A tug-of-war such as this is extremely frightening and damaging for Brian. Brian's father must have felt very threatened about losing Brian when you took him to California, just as you do now. Be as cooperative as you can and try to work out a plan with Brian's father that will provide your son with as much time as possible with his father. Perhaps Brian could spend the entire summer vacation and part of winter and spring vacations with his father, plus additional times, should his father be able to come to the mainland to see him during the school year.

If you and your ex-husband are unable to reach an agreement, I suggest that when you are in court you have your attorney request custody-visitation counseling in the conciliation court. In California, this service is mandatory whenever parents are disputing custody. A trained counselor-mediator meets with both parents, facilitates communication between them, assists them in exploring alternatives, helps parents focus on their children's needs, and, when parents are willing, assists them in reaching an amicable agreement regarding custody and visitation.

A Mother Is Concerned About Her Estranged Adolescent Becoming Pregnant

Dear Florence:

My teenage daughter Valerie is manipulating me and her father to get her way. Her father and I have been divorced for three years. Valerie is now seventeen and a senior in high school. She has always been strong-willed, but since the divorce she has become even more difficult. Until recently she was living with me. Then we had an argument about her boyfriend sleeping over and her cutting classes. Valerie left in a huff to go live with her father. He welcomed her with open arms and

and wouldn't back me up. I'm scared Valerie will get pregnant and that she won't finish high school. Is there anything I can do?

Signed

L———.

Dear L:

There may not be much you can do, since Valerie is no longer living with you. Parents are bound to have confrontations with their adolescent children. At this age, children strive to be independent and grown-up. They will test, strain, and often break rules and boundaries that their parents have set up for them, especially when parents are not working together and supporting the same values and goals. If Valerie can't get her way with you, she runs to her father. Rather than try to force her to come back to live with you at this time, concentrate on trying to help Valerie by enlisting her father's help.

It seems to me that both you and her father should be very concerned about Valerie getting pregnant and about her cutting classes. I suggest you write him a note expressing your concern in a straightforward manner. Tell him that you want him to work with you to help Valerie, and suggest a meeting to discuss these issues as parents. You could meet either alone or with a counselor or mediator. If he agrees to a meeting, then stick to the issues without put-downs or bringing up the past. An additional meeting should then be planned that includes Valerie. At the very least, Valerie and her boyfriend need information regarding birth control, if they don't have this information already. Planned Parenthood centers offer free examinations and birth control advice in most areas of the United States.

Regarding Valerie's education, I suggest that you and her father meet with the school counselor with Valerie present. In this way she will see that both of you are concerned that she gets a good education and attends classes regularly.

You cannot force Valerie's father to work with you on this,

but it is to be hoped that your conciliatory and nonthreatening approach will convince him that it is in his and Valerie's best interests to do so.

In addition to the above, I suggest you reach out and try to repair and improve your relationship with Valerie. She needs your love and guidance, even though she fights you at times. In order to be able to influence her, you need a closer relationship with her, but avoid pressuring her to live with you. As your relationship improves, she will probably be willing to spend time with you, but she should also spend time with her father, even if she returns to your home.

A Father Misses Time with His Adolescent Sons

Dear Florence:

I have been divorced for ten years. I have two teenage sons, fourteen and sixteen years old, who live with their mother. I am a very good father. I have always paid child support and have seen my sons regularly. They used to love to come with me on weekends, but lately they have been calling to cancel. They say they've got things to do. I get angry. I miss them. Should I force them to come? What should I do?

Signed

N———.

Dear N:

I sense your pain. I must tell you that this situation is a predictable one. Younger children's lives and activities revolve around their parents. However, as adolescents strive for independence, their peer group takes precedence, while time with parents takes a back seat. If you and their mother had remained married, your sons would still have had activities on weekends and would not have stayed home with you.

As far as what to do about this, I suggest that you plan your time with them around their activities. If they can't stay over with you for the entire weekend, perhaps they could spend part of it at your house. Another alternative would be to have them spend the weekend with you, coming and going for their activities as they desire. At times perhaps you and your sons could make plans that all of you would enjoy.

It would not be advisable for you to force them to come, even if you could. It would only make them resent you and want to spend less time with you.

An obvious way to see more of your sons is to have them live with you part of the time, not just on weekends or vacations. Here again, I wouldn't pressure them about living with you. It would be best to discuss this with their mother first. If she is in agreement then you could present this idea to your boys for discussion.

To put this into perspective, it won't be very many years until your sons will be living on their own without either you or their mother. Then you will want them to fit you into their schedules, even when they are grown, because they love you.

*

When a marriage comes to an end, even the coolest-headed parents are faced with difficult problems to solve, tremendous challenges to overcome, and many questions to ask. They have themselves and their own lives to worry about, they have their child(ren) to raise, and they have a potentially sensitive relationship with the other parent to develop and maintain.

The questions and answers discussed in this chapter reflect the pressures that so many parents feel, and some of the confused thinking that may result. It is my hope that the answers have given you some help, insight, and perspective, and will strengthen your resolve to cooperate with the other parent, as difficult as this may seem.

9

Where Help Can Be Found

On airplanes, flight attendants instruct passengers in the emergency use of oxygen masks should extreme loss of pressure occur in the cabin. They ask parents traveling with children to place the mask on themselves first, then to assist children with their masks. The reason is obvious. If a parent should lose consciousness, there would be no one to help the children.

The same concept applies to parents and children after separation and divorce. Parents need to take immediate steps to help themselves maintain balance and keep their sanity. If parents become unconscious of everything but their own pain, they lose the ability to consider their children's needs. These parents owe it to themselves and their children to get psychological help and/or legal advice, and create a support network of *some* kind that will help them come to terms with the situation. They need to resume their responsibility as parents and find the strength to stop behaving like angry children out of control.

Divorce does not have to be a Greek tragedy in which everyone dies. Everyone can live, and in time recover, heal, and do very well. The recovery process usually takes two or three years and may take longer. During this time, parents who have great difficulty coping need to seek help for themselves, so that they can take proper care of their children.

The children may need help also. It is amazing what a difference a few sessions with a counselor or therapist can make. The following true story (See *References*, 4) is an example

of how quickly a child can respond to and benefit from counseling and/or mediation, even in extremely difficult cases.

Halli was a bright, sensitive girl of almost eleven. Her parents and their attorneys were referred to me directly from the
courtroom where the parents were litigating over custody and
visitation issues. They had separated when Halli was seven
years old, and Halli's mother had remarried two years before.

During the first conference, Halli's mother, father, and
stepfather, as well as the parents' attorneys, were present. After I gave a brief explanation of the mediation process, the two
attorneys left and waited outside while I talked to the parents,
Martha and Hal. Martha began, "Halli refuses to go to see her
father. I haven't told her not to go. I can't push her out the
door." She stated that she was concerned for her child and had
been taking Halli to a child psychologist for the past month.
"Her psychologist feels she shouldn't be forced until she can
work it out. I want her to see her father."

I asked Martha if Halli had given her any reason why she
did not wish to see her father, and she replied, "She's mad at
him for leaving her and me. Our life-style was to stay married
and not to have any extramarital sex. Halli is upset about Hal's
constant changes in girlfriends. When they break up, Halli believes he is hurting them the way he hurt me." Martha believed
that Hal should wait until Halli had accepted the divorce and
not force her to go with him. "I want them both to feel good
about it," she said. She indicated her concern about the negative consequences of the divorce on her child, because Halli had
seen and heard a lot of verbal and physical abuse between Hal
and Martha.

Hal told me that he loved Halli very much and wanted
to share his life with her. "I can't work on my relationship with
her if I don't have any contact. I don't want to wait a long
time to see her. They don't encourage her to see me. Separate-
ness doesn't lead to resolving this situation. I don't have a flow
of several women. I lived first with one woman and now
another woman, whom I plan to marry—only two different
women." Hal added with great feeling, "I want to see my

daughter on a regular basis. If I get to spend time with her I am confident that we will be able to work it out. If I don't get to see her regularly, I believe a change of custody is necessary now, otherwise this will keep happening over and over again. I'll give Martha the same visitation rights that she would give me."

I talked to them about their mutual responsibility for the problem, about the importance of both of them cooperating to correct the situation for Halli's sake, and about the negative consequences for children when a serious rift develops between a parent and child. I suggested that Halli be included in the mediation process, and also presented the possibility of Hal's participating in some counseling sessions with Halli and her psychologist. Hal was negative about participating in counseling, as the psychologist had recommended that Halli not be forced to see her father, but both parents agreed to return with Halli the following week.

On the day of their appointment the three of them came to my office. I explained the purpose of the meeting to Halli, then asked her parents to wait outside while I interviewed her alone. Most children sit quietly and wait for my first question before they begin telling me about their situation, but Halli immediately began airing her complaints and resentments about her father. "He goes from lady to lady even when he was married to my mother." I asked her how she knew this and she said her mother had told her so. Halli continued, "If I start with that I will have a terrible life. This lady will be left like a dead rose." Halli's eyes filled with tears as she told me that her father had punched her mother in the stomach when she was in her mother's womb. Her mother had told her so.

Halli said, "When I was five years old, my father punished me by putting me to bed because he wanted me to clean my room. He never did love me. He lied on the court papers." I asked Halli how she knew this and she told me that she and her mother had read them and that her father had contradicted himself.

Halli said she never believed her father loved her. "When

he left I thought he would come back but he didn't. If he really would have loved me, he wouldn't have left me." She added, "It's a lie that my mother's trying to put words in my mouth."

I asked Halli what made her decide not to see her father, and she replied, "We went away for the weekend to a hotel and my father had sex with that lady. I know because I came into the room and she had her bikini top unfastened. After that I didn't want to see him anymore. I think he's trying to threaten my mother by taking her to court. He doesn't want to see me. He has no love. He thinks sex is love. He never took care of me when I was a baby. Do you get the point?"

I asked Halli what the worst thing was that her father had done to her and she replied, "He left me. It's in my heart and in my mother's and it never comes out until we talk to someone." I asked Halli where she felt the hurt in her body and she replied, "It makes me want to cry. It feels like, you know, when you're cold." She shivered. "Like that." Halli continued, "Every day he'd beat my mother up. I would see him punch her."

I asked Halli if she would give me permission to share what we talked about with her father, and Halli replied, "Good. I want to see how he will react to the lies he's telling and to what I say, and what he's going to do when his girlfriend is in here." She added, "I don't want to see my father's face. I didn't look at him in the waiting room. I want him to know what it's like to be hurt. He has never been hurt. He left my mother and left another woman like a dead rose. He'll leave this lady too." I asked Halli if she thought she could ever forgive her father for hurting her, and she replied, "I can never forgive him for the way he hurt my heart."

I asked Halli if she had told her father about the way she felt, and Halli replied, "I've never told my father all these things."

Instead of bringing both parents and Mike, Halli's stepfather, and Kay, Hal's friend, in at this point, which I normally would have done, I decided to bring in only Hal so that Halli and her father could have a chance to be together alone. I also believed it would be easier for Hal to accept Halli's feelings if Martha were not in the room. I explained this to Martha and she accepted my decision. When Hal came into the room, Halli rose from her seat and went to the far end of the room, turning her back on him. I explained to Hal that I would be summarizing Halli's feelings and that it might be very difficult for him to hear what Halli had to say. I also explained that feelings don't have a right or wrong, they just are the way they are, and that sometimes when feelings are expressed they come loose. They can then change and a closer relationship can develop. I summarized what Halli and I had talked about and when I finished, Hal told Halli how amazed and sad he was to hear how much hurt he had caused her.

Halli waited outside while I discussed the situation with the adults. Again, I strongly suggested that Hal take part in at least one session with Halli's psychologist. He reluctantly agreed to give it a try and to postpone further visitation until after his meeting with the psychologist. All present agreed to return in one month to evaluate what progress had been made.

One month later, Halli walked into my office smiling broadly. "Things are working out," she announced. "I'm seeing my father again. I might forgive him. After we talked about it he knows what I want and I know what he wants."

I asked Halli, "What do you want?"

Halli replied, "When I'm with him I don't want him to sleep with any ladies. I want them to have separate beds."

I asked Halli, "What does your father want?"

Halli replied, smiling, "He wants to see me. He wants a better relationship with me. He wants me to forgive him. He found out he hurt me more than he thought he did. He apologized and I forgave him."

Again Halli gave permission for me to share what we talked about with her parents. Martha told me that a big change had taken place in Halli. "She is so happy now."

Hal announced to everyone present that he was planning to get married that summer and he wanted Halli to attend his wedding. Halli smiled approvingly. I asked Halli jokingly,

"Then will it be all right for your father to sleep with Kay?" And without hesitation Halli smiled and answered, "Yes!"

Children are extremely resilient. They can heal rather quickly once the pressure is eased or their situation changes for the better, as in the case of Halli. Usually, a resolution between their parents that brings an end to hostilities and fighting and some constructive cooperation will restore a kernel of security in their lives. Adults need a wider and more complex support network. Family and friends can help, but sometimes the person is too isolated, or the problem lies so deep that the trained care of a professional is best. At such times divorcing adults owe it to themselves—and their children—to seek out and use the resources that have been developed in their community.

On the following pages I have listed various kinds of services available to separated, divorcing, or divorced parents. These include emergency services, psychological services, legal services, parent support groups, conciliation courts and family court mediation services, and conflict resolution and mediation associations and agencies. In a separate section I have listed several books that I refer to for guidance in my day to day work, books that I believe could help you too.

Emergency Services for Families

Immediate help for serious problems such as spouse battering, child abuse, child molestation and rape can be found through

— local police departments (dial 911 in an emergency)

— shelters for battered spouses

— social workers

Help for psychological disturbances can be obtained through local county mental health agencies.

For problems with addictions, self-help groups such as Alcoholics Anonymous, Narcotics Anonymous and Gamblers Anonymous are available in many communities for treating specific problems and are listed in the yellow pages under "Social Service Organizations."

Local hotlines and specialized social services are also listed under "Social Service Organizations" in the Yellow Pages. Additional information and referrals can be obtained through the Alliance of Information and Referral Systems, 47 South Pennsylvania Street, Indianapolis, IN 46208, (317) 637-6101. Some national hotlines include:

— Child Abuse: Childhelp *1-800-4-A-CHILD*

— Sexual and Physical Abuse: National Council on Child Abuse and Family Violence *1-800-222-2000*

— Domestic Violence: House of Ruth *202-842-0192*

— Suicide Counseling: National Save-A-Life League *212-492-4067*

In addition to these resources, many clergymen and women are specially trained in pastoral counseling and can be of assistance in providing counseling themselves or in giving referrals for help elsewhere.

Psychological Services

The following professional associations can provide information regarding trained marriage, family, and child counselors; social workers; and psychologists and psychiatrists in your area.

American Association of Marriage and Family Therapy
1717 K Street NW
Washington DC 20006   *(202) 429-1825*

American Psychiatric Association
1400 K Street NW
Washington DC 20006   *(202) 682-6000*

American Psychological Association
1200 17th Street NW
Washington DC 20006   *(202) 955-7600*

Association of Family and Conciliation Courts
c/o OSHU Department of Psychiatry
3181 Sam Jackson Road
Portland OR 97201   *(503) 225-8145*

Family Service Association of America
254 West 31st Street
New York NY 10010   *(212) 967-2740*

National Association of Social Workers, Inc.
4545 Eighth Avenue
New York NY 10016   *(212) 947-5000*

Legal Services

Referrals for legal advice can be obtained from

— local county bar associations

— the American Bar Association (750 North Lake Shore Drive, Chicago, IL 60611, *(312) 988-5000)*

— local yellow pages listed under "Divorce"

I suggest that parents ask for a referral to a *family law* attorney. Parents are wise to shop around until they find an attorney whose goal is to help parents settle their differences rather than to litigate, especially when litigation may not be in the children's and parents' best interests. There are many fine and ethical attorneys who realize that family law is not like criminal or corporate or other law. When the divorce is over, the litigants (parents) have to work together regarding their children. It is therefore important that attorneys try to deescalate the conflict whenever possible and try to help parents reach a mutually beneficial settlement of their differences.

In some towns or counties, lawyers establish free or inexpensive legal clinics for those who cannot afford private attorneys. These can be found in local Yellow Pages listed under "Legal Clinics." Another source of legal help is law schools that frequently provide *pro bono* services.

Parent Support Groups

Fathers' Rights of America
P.O. Box 7596
Van Nuys CA 91409   *(818) 789-4435*

Joint Custody Association
10606 Wilkins Avenue
Los Angeles CA 90024   *(213) 475-5352*

Mothers Without Custody
P.O. Box 76
Sudbury MA 01766

Parents Without Partners International Office
8807 Colesville Road
Silver Springs MD 20910   *(301) 588-9354*

Stepfamily Association of America
602 East Joppa Road
Towson MD 21204   *(301) 823-7570*

Stepfamily Association of America
California Chapter
550 St. Charles Drive
Thousand Oaks CA 91360   *(805) 495-8435*

Conciliation Courts and Family Court Mediation Services

Below is a partial list of conciliation courts and family court mediation services. This list is incomplete, since new courts are continually being formed; the listing for California is extensive as these services are most developed in this state. To find the current status of conciliation courts in your area, inquire at your local courthouse.

ALASKA

Anchorage   *(907) 264-0461*
Superior Court-Trial Courts
Domestic Relations,
   Children's Matters
303 K Street
Anchorage AK 99501

ARIZONA

Phoenix   *(602) 262-3296*
Conciliation Court of
   Maricopa County
Superior Court Building
201 West Jefferson Street,
   Second Floor
Phoenix AZ 85003

Tucson   *(602) 792-6344*
Conciliation Court of
   Pima County
177 North Church
Tucson AZ 85701

CALIFORNIA (listed by county)

Alameda   *(415) 272-6030*
Child Custody Mediation Office
Alameda County Family
   Conciliation Court
1221 Oak Street
Oakland CA 94612

Child Custody   *(415) 881-6146*
   Mediation Office
Hall of Justice Third Floor
24405 Amador Street
Hayward CA 94544

Alpine   *(916) 694-2281*
Child Custody Investigations/
   Mediation Office
Superior Court of Alpine County
P.O. Box 276
Markleeville CA 96120

Amador   (209) 223-6387
Child Custody Investigation/
  Mediation Office
Amador County Probation Office
108 Court Street
Jackson CA 95642

Butte   (916) 534-4793
Child Custody
  Investigations Office
Family Conciliation Court
2243 Del Oro Avenue
Oroville CA 95965

Calaveras   (209) 745-4252
Child Custody Mediation Office
Welfare Department
891 Mountain Ranch Road,
Government Center
San Andreas CA 95249

Colusa   (916) 458-5871
Child Custody Investigations/
  Mediation Office
Colusa County Probation Office
Courthouse, 546 Jay Street
Colusa CA 95932

Contra Costa   (415) 372-2681
Child Custody Mediation Office
Family Conciliation Court
928 Main Street
Martinez CA 94553

Del Norte   (707) 464-7215
Child Custody Investigations/
  Mediation Office
Probation Department
County of Del Norte Courthouse
Crescent City CA 95531

El Dorado   (916) 626-2431
Child Custody Mediation Office
El Dorado County
  Superior Court
495 Main Street
Placerville CA 95667

Fresno   (209) 488-3241
Child Custody Investigations/
  Mediation Office
Family Court Services
2100 Tulare, Room 220
Fresno CA 93721

Glenn   (916) 934-3308
Child Custody Investigations/
  Mediation Office
Office of Conciliation, Glenn
  County Probation Office
Court House, Room 200
Willows CA 95988

Humboldt   (707) 445-7401
Child Custody Investigations/
  Mediation Office
Humboldt County
  Probation Department
2002 Harrison Avenue
Eureka CA 95501

Imperial   (619) 352-6302
Child Custody Mediation Office
Valley Psychological and
  Counseling Association
107 South Fifth Street, Suite 218
El Centro CA 92243

Inyo   *(714) 878-2441, ext.* 2217
Child Custody Investigations/
  Mediation Office
Probation Department of
  Inyo County
P.O. Box Drawer U
Independence CA 93526

Kern   *(805) 861-3464*
Child Custody Investigations/
  Mediation Office
Family Court Services Unit
Kern County Probation
  Department
P.O. Box 3309, Station A
Bakersfield CA 93385-3309

Kings   *(209) 582-3211, ext.* 2850
Child Custody Investigations/
  Mediation Office
Kings County Probation,
  Government Center
1400 West Lacey Boulevard
Hanford CA 93230

Lake   *(707) 263-2232*
Child Custody Investigation/
  Mediation Office
Lake County Superior Court
255 North Forbes Street
Lakeport CA 95453

Lassen   *(916) 257-8311, ext.* 119
Child Custody Investigations/
  Mediation Office
Lassen County Probation
  Department
220 South Lasen
Susanville CA 96130

Los Angeles   *(213) 974-5524*
Child Custody Mediation Office
Conciliation Court
111 North Hill Street, Room 241
Los Angeles CA 90012

Madera   *(209) 675-7739*
Child Custody Investigations/
  Mediation Office
Probation Office,
  Madera County
209 West Yosemite Avenue
Madera CA 93637

Marin   *(415) 499-6612*
Child Custody Mediation Office
Marin County Probation
  Department
Conciliation Program
Civic Center, Hall of Justice,
  Room 163
San Raphael CA 94903

Mariposa   *(209) 966-3612*
Child Custody Investigations/
  Mediation Office
P.O. Box 76
Mariposa CA 95338

Mendocino   *(707) 463-4484*
Child Custody Mediation Office
Mendocino County
  Superior Court #1
Courthouse
Ukiah CA 95482

Merced   *(209) 385-7569*
Child Custody Investigations/
  Mediation Office
Probation Department
2150 "M" Street
Merced CA 95340

Modoc   *(916) 233-3939, ext. 324*
Child Custody Investigations/
  Mediation Office
County Probation Department
201 South Court
Alturas CA 96101

Mono   *(619) 932-7911, ext. 250*
Child Custody Investigations/
  Mediation Office
Probation Department
P.O. Box 596
Bridgeport CA 93517

Monterey   *(408) 424-0329/424-6464*
Child Custody Mediation Office
P.O. Box 414
Salinas CA 93902

Napa   *(707) 253-4206*
Child Custody Mediation Office
Napa County Conciliation Court
825 Brown Street, Third Floor
Napa CA 94559

Nevada   *(916) 272-6231*
Child Custody Mediation Office
Nevada County
  Conciliation Court
11721 Nevada City Highway,
  Suite 2
Grass Valley CA 92945

Orange   *(714) 834-6507*
Child Custody Investigations/
  Mediation Office
Family Conciliation
  Court Services
700 Civic Center Drive, West
Santa Ana CA 92701

Placer   *(916) 783-5003*
Child Custody Investigations/
  Mediation Office
Placer County Superior Court
700 Sunrise Boulevard, Suite H
Roseville CA 95661

Plumas   *(916) 283-1860*
Child Custody Investigations/
  Mediation Office
Plumas County Probation
Box 258
Quincy CA 95971

Riverside   *(714) 787-2788*
Child Custody Mediation Office,
  Family Conciliation Court
4050 Main Street, Room 235
Riverside CA 92501

Sacramento   *(916) 440-5633*
Child Custody Investigations/
  Mediation Office
Family Court Services
800 Ninth Street, First Floor
Sacramento CA 95814

San Benito   *(408) 637-5829*
Child Custody Investigations/
  Mediation Office
San Benito County
  Probation Department
440 Fifth Street,
  Room 105, Courthouse
Hollister CA 95023

San Bernardino   *(714) 387-3912*
Child Custody Investigations/
  Mediation Office
Family Court Services
351 North Arrowhead Avenue,
Courthouse, Room 200
San Bernardino CA 92404

San Diego   *(714) 236-2681*
Child Custody Investigations/
   Mediation Office
Family Counseling Services of
   the Superior Court
210 West Ash
San Diego CA 92101

Out-of-county requests to:
San Diego County
   Probation Department
(714) 560-3202
Civil Investigation Unit
2901 Meadowlark Drive
San Diego CA 92123

San Francisco   *(415) 558-4186*
Child Custody Mediation Office
Family Court Service Office
City Hall, Room 463
San Francisco CA 94102

San Joaquin   *(209) 944-2101*
Child Custody Investigations/
   Mediation Office
San Joaquin County
   Superior Court
Courthouse, Room 370
Stockton CA 95202

San Luis Obispo   *(805) 549-5423*
Child Custody Mediation Office
Family Court Services
1070 Palm Street
San Luis Obispo CA 93401

San Mateo   *(415) 363-4561*
Child Custody Mediation Office
Family Conciliation Court
Hall of Justice and Records
401 Marshall Street
Redwood City CA 94063

Santa Barbara   *(805) 963-6150*
Child Custody Mediation Office
Superior Court
1100 Anacapa Street
Santa Barbara CA 93101

Santa Clara   *(408) 299-3741*
Child Custody Mediation Office
Family Court Services
161 North First Street
San Jose CA 95113

Santa Cruz   *(408) 423-1955*
Child Custody Mediation Office
Family Mediation Service
345 Church
Santa Cruz CA 95060

Shasta   *(916) 255-5707/225-5106*
Child Custody Investigations/
   Mediation Office
Probate and Family
   Court Services
1558 West Street, Suite 1
Redding CA 96001

Sierra   *(916) 289-3277*
Child Custody Mediation Office
Sierra County Probation
   Department
P.O. Box 67
Downieville CA 95936

Siskiyou   *(916) 842-5440*
Child Custody Investigations/
   Mediation Office
Siskiyou County Probation Office
322 West Center Street, #6
Yreka CA 96097

Solano   *(707) 429-6547*
Child Custody Mediation Office
Hall of Justice
600 Union Avenue, Chamber B
Fairfield CA 94533

Sonoma   *(707) 527-2765*
Child Custody Mediation Office
Superior Court
3033 Cleveland Avenue,
   Suite 107
Santa Rosa CA 95401

Child Custody Mediation Office
(707) 527-2765
Conciliation Court, Room 107J,
Hall of Justice
600 Administration Drive
Santa Rosa CA 95401

Stanislaus   *(209) 571-6302*
Child Custody Investigations/
   Mediation Office
Superior Court
P.O. Box 3488
Modesto CA 95353

Sutter   *(916) 741-7307*
Child Custody Mediation Office
Sutter/Yuba Sheriff's Department
1077 Civic Center Boulevard
Yuba City CA 95991

Tehama   *(916) 527-2170*
Child Custody Investigations/
   Mediation Office
Family Conciliation Court
Tehama County Courthouse,
Room 23
P.O. Box 1315
Red Bluff CA 96080

Trinity   *(916) 623-1201*
Child Custody Mediation Office
Superior Court of Trinity County
P.O. Box 1188
Weaverville CA 96093

Tulare   *(209) 733-6247*
Child Custody Investigations/
   Mediation Office
Tulare County Probation
   Department
Courthouse, Room 206
Visalia CA 93291

Tuolumne   *(209) 533-5666*
Child Custody Mediation Office
Tuolumne County
   Probation Office
2 South Green Street
Sonora CA 95370

Ventura   *(805) 654-2671/654-2672*
Child Custody Investigations/
   Mediation Office
Superior Court, Ventura County
800 South Victoria Avenue
Ventura CA 93009

Yolo   *(916) 666-8010*
Child Custody
   Investigations Office
County Probation Department
218 West Beamer
Woodland CA 95695
(Mediation referred to outside
agencies)

Yuba   *(916) 674-6431*
Child Custody Investigations/
   Mediation Office
Probation Department of
   Yuba County
215 Fifth Street
Marysville CA 95901

CONNECTICUT

West Hartford   *(203) 566-7973*
Family Division, Superior Court,
State of Connecticut
28 Grand Street
Hartford CT 06106

FLORIDA

Fort Lauderdale   *(305) 765-4012*
Family Conciliation Unit,
   Circuit Court
507 SE Sixth Street
Fort Lauderdale FL 33301

Miami   *(305) 375-1650*
Dade County Family
   Mediation Unit
73 West Flagler Street
Miami FL 33130

HAWAII

Honolulu   *(808) 548-7661*
Family Court, First Circuit
P.O. Box 3498
Judiciary Building
Honolulu HI 96811

Maui   *(808) 244-2290*
Family Court, Second Circuit
2145 Kaohu Street
P.O. Box 969
Wailuku Maui HI 96793

ILLINOIS

Chicago   *(312) 353-7350*
Conciliation Service
175 West Jackson Boulevard
Chicago IL 60604

MARYLAND

Baltimore   *(301) 333-3799*
Family Court Mediation Services
503 Court House West
100 North Calvert Street
Baltimore MD 21262

MICHIGAN

Detroit   *(313) 224-5266*
Counseling Service of
   Wayne County Circuit Court
Third Judicial Circuit
   of Michigan
500 Cadillac Tower
Detroit MI 48226

MINNESOTA

Minneapolis   *(612) 348-7556*
Domestic Relations Division
A503 Government Center
Minneapolis MN 55487

MONTANA

Kalispell   *(406) 752-5300 x349*
Family Court Services
723 Fifth Avenue East
Kalispell MT 59901

NEBRASKA

Lincoln   *(402) 471-7429*
The Conciliation Court
555 South Tenth
Lincoln NE 68508

Omaha   *(402) 444-7168*
The Conciliation Court
Hall of Justice
17th and Farman Street
Omaha NE 68183

NEW JERSEY

Morristown   *(201) 744-7632*
Morristown Family and
    Mediation Service
95 Mount Kemble Avenue
Morristown NJ 07960

NEW MEXICO

Albuquerque   *(505) 841-7409*
Albuquerque Superior
    Court Clinic
Albuquerque NM 87103

OREGON

Portland   *(503) 248-3189*
Family Services
Court of Domestic Relations
Multnomah County Courthouse,
Room 315
Portland OR 97204

Port Orchard   *(206) 876-7140*
Family Court
Kitsap County Superior Court
614 Division Street
Port Orchard OR 98366

Salem   *(503) 588-5088*
Marion County Family Court
Conciliation Services Division
3030 Center Street
Salem OR 97301

WASHINGTON

Everett   *(206) 259-0031*
Family Court Division
Court of Domestic Relations
2801 Tenth Street
Everett WA 98201

Seattle   *(206) 583-4690*
Family Court
W-364 King County Courthouse
Seattle WA 98104

Tacoma   *(206)756-0606*
Family Court
5501 Sixth Avenue
Tacoma WA 98402

Vancouver   *(206) 699-2326*
Clark County Family Court
711 West 12th Street
Vancouver WA 98660

WISCONSIN

Madison   *(608) 266-4607*
Dane County Family Court
Counseling Service
City-County Building, Room 106
Madison WI 53709

CANADA

Edmonton (403) 427-8337	*Ontario* (416) 525-2830
Edmonton Family Court	Unified Family Court
500 Century Place	100 James Street South
9803 - 102A Avenue,	Hamilton, Ontario
Edmonton, Alberta	Canada L8P 2Z3
Canada T5J 3A6	

Conflict Resolution and Mediation Associations and Agencies

If there are no court-connected concilliation or mediation services in your area, it may be possible to find information regarding private mediation services by contacting the agencies below.

Academy of Family Mediators
P.O. Box 4686
Greenwich CT 06830   (203) 629-8049

American Arbitration Association
140 West 51st Street
New York NY 10020   (212) 484-4000

American Association for Mediated Divorce
5435 Balboa Boulevard, Suite 208
Encino CA 91316   (818) 986-6953

American Association of Family Counselors and Mediators
Davis Professional Park
5225 Route 347, Suite 25
Port Jefferson Stn NY 11776 (516) 589-9482

American Bar Association
Special Committee on Alternative Means of
    Dispute Resolution
1800 M Street, NW
Washington DC 20036   (202) 331-2200

Association of Family Conciliation Courts
c/o OSHU, Department of Psychiatry
3181 Sam Jackson Road
Portland OR 97201   *(503) 220-5790*

Center for Community Justice
918 - 16th Street, NW
Washington DC 20006   *(202) 296-2565*

Center for Dispute Resolution
1900 Wazee Street, Suite 311
Denver CO 80202   *(303) 295-2244*

Divorce Mediation Institute
1580 North Northwest Highway, Suite 111
Park Ridge IL 60068   *(312) 696-6023*

Divorce Mediators, Inc.
10604 Wilkins Avenue
Los Angeles CA 90024   *(213) 474-2259*

Family Mediation Association of Maryland
10605 Concord Street
Kensington MD 20895   *(301) 946-3400*

Family Mediation Center
1020 Taylor, Suite 845
Portland OR 97201   *(503) 248-9740*

Family Mediation Service
6233 Soquel Drive
Aptos CA 95003   *(408) 476-8962*

Family Counseling and Mediation Services
P.O. Box 40
Pacific Palisades CA 90272   *(213) 459-5633*

National Council for Children's Rights
2001 O Street
Washington DC 20036   *(202) 223-6227*

Suggested Reading List

Books About Children of Divorce

Child Custody Mediation: Techniques for Counselors, Attorneys and Parents, Florence Bienenfeld. Palo Alto, CA: Science and Behavior Books, 1983.

This practical guide describes the entire mediation process in a simple way and offers parents and counselors many suggestions for resolving difficult child custody disputes.

The Day the Loving Stopped, Julie List. New York: Sea View Books, 1980.

A devastating account of the typical divorce and its effect on children.

Parents Book About Divorce, Richard A. Gardner. New York: Doubleday and Co., 1977.

In this book, a psychiatrist gives realistic guidance for parents who are having trouble with their children because of divorce. Dr. Gardner offers a positive approach and a comprehensive treatment of complex issues.

Surviving the Breakup, Judith S. Wallerstein and Joan Berlin Kelly. New York: Basic Books, 1980.

This book has valuable information on the impact of divorce on children, based on a longitudinal study of children of divorce.

Your Child's Self-Esteem, Dorothy Corkille Brings. New York: Dolphin Books, 1975.

This book is not about divorce per se, but its author's insights into child behavior and development will help parents deal with their children in difficult times, especially divorce.

Books for Children of Divorce

Children's Book About Divorce, Richard A. Gardner New York: Jason Aronson, 1970.

This book, quickly becoming a classic, is written for children, but will help parents anticipate questions and problems.

The Divorce Workbook, Sally B. Ives. Burlington, VT: Waterfront Books, 1985.

A useful therapeutic tool to help children communicate about their feelings.

How to Get It Together When Your Parents Are Coming Apart, Arlene Kramer Richards and Irene Willis. New York: David McKay, 1976.

This book aims at helping teenagers deal with their parents' divorce.

My Mom and Dad Are Getting a Divorce, Florence Bienenfeld. Available only through EMC Corporation, 300 York Avenue, St. Paul, MN 55101. $6.20, including postage.

Although this book is written for children from four to twelve years old, parents, teachers, counselors, attorneys, and judges will also find it useful. Illustrated in color, this book expresses the feelings of children whose parents are going through divorce. It will help children, parents, and professionals deal with those feelings. Endorsed by the Association of Family Conciliation Courts.

Books About Shared Custody

Joint Custody and Co-Parenting Handbook, Miriam Galper. Philadelphia: Running Press, 1980.

A series of reports from the trenches by parents who opted for joint custody arrangements in the 1970s.

Joint Custody and Shared Parenting, edited by Jay Folberg. Washington, DC: BNA Books, 1984.

A compilation of writings on the legal, social, and practical aspects of joint custody; including a survey of custody across the fifty states, with particular emphasis on joint custody and co-parenting.

Mom's House, Dad's House, Isolina Ricci. New York: Macmillan, 1980.

This sensitively written book articulates practical and systematic guidelines for parents who are contemplating divorce, are involved in divorce litigation, or are already divorced. Dr. Ricci offers persuasive arguments to support the pioneering idea that divorced parents can cooperate and build two homes for their children, even when they are not on friendly terms.

Sharing Parenthood After Divorce: An Enlightened Child Custody Guide for Mothers, Fathers, and Kids, Ciji Ware. New York: Viking Press, 1982.

This book shows how divorcing couples can cooperate as parents after divorce, sharing both responsibilities and the pleasures of parenthood.

The Custody Handbook, Persia Wooley. New York: Summit Books, 1979.

This book surveys many types of child custody arrangements, with special emphasis on sharing responsibility for children after their parents' divorce.

The Disposable Parent: The Case for Joint Custody, Mel Roman and William Haddad. New York: Holt, Rinehart and Winston, 1978.

The authors throw down the gauntlet, challenging the opinions of armies of "either/or" custody experts who claim sole custody best serves the interests of children after their parents' divorce. The studies presented directly contradict this notion.

Books About Divorce

Creative Divorce, Mel Krantzler. New York: M. Evans and Co., 1974.

The Divorce Experience, Morton Hunt and Bernice Hunt. New York: McGraw-Hill, 1977.

Books for Divorced Mothers

Life After Marriage, Mary Ann Singleton. New York: Stein and Day, 1974.

Women in Transition: A Feminist Handbook on Separation and Divorce. New York: Scribner's, 1975.

Books for Divorced Fathers

Father Power, Henry Biller and Dennis Meredith. New York: David McKay, 1974.

Weekend Fathers, Gerald A. and Myrna Silver. Stratford Press, 1981.

Who Will Raise the Children? New Options for Fathers (and Mothers), James A. Levine. Philadelphia: Lippincott, 1976.

101 Ways to Be a Long Distance Super Dad, George Newman. Mountain View, CA: Blossom Valley Press, P.O. Box 4044, 1981.

Books About Stepparenting

The Half Parent, Brenda Maddox. New York: M. Evans and Co., 1975.

Stepfamilies: Myths and Realities, Emily Visher and John Visher. New York: Lyle Stuart Books, 1980.

The Successful Step-Parent, Helen Thomson. New York: Harper and Row, 1966.

Books About Single Parenting

Creative Survival for Single Mothers, Persia Wooley. Milbrea, CA: Celestial Arts, 1975.

Part-Time Father, Edith Atkin and Estelle Rubin. New York: Vanguard Press, 1976.

The Divorced Mother's Guide, Lynn Forman. Berkeley, CA: Berkeley Publishing Corp., 1974.

Enjoying Single Parenthood, Bryan M. Knight. New York: Van Nostrand Reinhold, 1980.

References

1. *Marriage and Divorce Today Newsletter*, report of a presentation made by Deborah Ann Leupnitz, Ph.D., to the Sixty-second Annual Meeting of the Orthopsychiatric Association, New York City, May 6, 1985.

2. Frederick W. Ilfeld, Jr., M.D., Holly Zingale Ilfeld, M.A., and John R. Alexander, J.D., "Does Joint Custody Work? A First Look at Outcome Data of Relitigation," *American Journal of Psychiatry*, January 1982.

3. The original series of questions and answers appeared in the *Independent Journal* of Santa Monica, California, as a public service weekly column, entitled "For Better or Worse" during 1979, 1980, and 1981. The series of questions and answers in this section have been adapted from that original series.

4. Florence Bienenfeld, "How Child Custody Mediation Can Help Children," in *Family Therapy News*, July/August 1983.

Bibliography

Bienenfeld, Florence. *Child Custody Mediation: Techniques for Counselors, Attorneys and Parents*. Palo Alto, CA: Science and Behavior Books, 1983.

Bienenfeld, Florence. *My Mom and Dad Are Getting a Divorce*. St. Paul, MN: EMC Corp., 1980, repr. 1984.

Bienenfeld, Florence, and Elayne Gayman Kardener. Pamphlet. "Twenty Questions Divorcing Parents Ask About Their Children." Portland, OR: Association of Family Conciliation Courts (c/o Oregon Health Sciences University), 1982.

Drapkin, Robin, and Florence Bienenfeld. "The Power of Including Children in the Mediation Process." *Journal of Divorce*, 1985.

Jacobson, Doris. "Step-Family Interaction and Child Adjustment." Unpublished final report of a National Institute of Mental Health research study, 1984.

Lachkar, Joan. "Courts Beware: Narcissistic/Borderline Couples, Implications for Mediators." *Conciliation Courts Review*, 1986.

Ricci, Isolina. *Mom's House/Dad's House*. New York: Macmillan, 1980.

Wallerstein, Judith S., and Joan Berlin Kelly. *Surviving the Breakup*. New York: Basic Books, 1980.

INDEX

Use This Handy Order Form
for Your *SPECIAL DISCOUNT*
on Hunter House
PSYCHOLOGY BOOKS

ALL MIGHTY: A Study of the God Complex in Western Man by Horst E. Richter, Ph.D.
The obsession with power and the denial of suffering in Western civilization. A profoundly influential book in contemporary moral and political thought.
Hard Cover   320 pages $19.95

COUPLES IN COLLUSION: The Unconscious Dimension in Partner Relationships by Jürg Willi, M.D.
Explores the unconscious agreement between partners to avoid *real* areas of conflict. Provides a model to integrate different therapeutic approaches.
Soft Cover   288 pages $11.95

DYNAMICS OF COUPLES THERAPY: Understanding the Potential of the Couple/Therapist Triangle by Jürg Willi, M.D.
Couples therapy is explained in terms of the psychological involvement of the therapist with the couple. Includes a detailed case study.
Soft Cover   288 pages $11.95

THE ENABLER: When Helping Harms the Ones You Love by Angelyn Miller
Co-dependency is not limited to families involved with alcohol or drugs. Enabling behavior actually perpetuates the problems of the people the enabler appears to be helping.
Soft Cover   160 pages $6.95   (July, 1988)*

HEALTHY AGING: What We Know, What We Can Do
by Joseph Bonner, Ph.D. and William Harris
Exciting advances in biology tell us more than ever about the nature of the aging process, and the lifestyle habits that slow it down or speed it up.
Hard Cover   272 pages $11.95   20 Illustrations   (August, 1988)*

INTRANCE: Fundamental Psychological Patterns of the Inner and Outer World
by C. J. Schuurman, Ph.D.
Reaching individuation through introspection and analysis of deepest values.
Soft Cover   160 pages $9.95

LSD PSYCHOTHERAPY by Stanislav Grof, M.D.
The scientifically complete source of information on the history, results, and significance of LSD research. 52 plates in full color.
Hard Cover   352 pages   Illustrated $29.95

TRAUMA IN THE LIVES OF CHILDREN: Crisis and Stress Management Techniques for Teachers, Counselors, and Student Service Professionals by Kendall Johnson, Ph.D.
When bad things happen to children, much of the responsibility for dealing with the effects of trauma and crises falls on school and child welfare professionals. A practical guide.
Soft Cover   288 pages $12.95   (October, 1988)*

WRITING FROM WITHIN: A Step-By-Step Guide to Writing Your Life's Stories
by Bernard Selling
Takes the beginning writer on a voyage that brings the past back to life as vivid personal stories. A guide to writing techniques and to preserving one's own history.
Soft Cover   240 pages $9.95   (July, 1988)*
Classroom Edition $12.95   Available now

* These books may be ordered and paid for in advance; they will be shipped when specified.
Prices Subject to Change Without Notice
See Over for Ordering and Discounts

Add postage and handling at $2.00 for one book and $0.50 for every additional book. Canadian orders: $3.00 first book, $.50 each additional.
Please allow 6 to 8 weeks for delivery.

Name _____

Street/Number _____

City/State _____ Zip _____

PLEASE SEND ME:

ALL MIGHTY	_____ @ $19.95	_____
COUPLES IN COLLUSION	_____ @ $11.95	_____
DYNAMICS OF COUPLES THERAPY	_____ @ $11.95	_____
THE ENABLER	_____ @ $6.95	_____
HEALTHY AGING	_____ @ $17.95	_____
INTRANCE	_____ @ $9.95	_____
LSD PSYCHOTHERAPY	_____ @ $29.95	_____
TRAUMA IN THE LIVES OF CHILDREN	_____ @ $12.95	_____
WRITING FROM WITHIN	_____ @ $9.95	_____
WRITING FROM WITHIN Classroom Edition	_____ @ $12.95	_____

TOTAL		$_____
DISCOUNT AT _____%	**LESS**	$(_____
TOTAL COST OF BOOKS		$_____
Shipping & Handling		$_____
California Residents add Sales Tax		$_____
TOTAL AMOUNT ENCLOSED		$_____

( ) **Cash**   ( ) **Check**
( ) **Check here to receive our catalog of books**

Please complete and mail to:
HUNTER HOUSE INC., PUBLISHERS
PO Box 847, Claremont, CA 91711, USA

If you don't use this offer—give it to a friend!

CHARTING YOUR WAY THRU' PMS by Virginia M. Fontana et. al.
A woman's appointment book and planning guide. Charting your menstrual symptoms is the only reliable way to diagnose PMS.
Soft Cover   *64 pages*   *Illustrated*   *$2.95*

EXCLUSIVELY FEMALE: A Nutrition Guide for Better Menstrual Health
by Linda Ojeda, Ph.D.
Nutrition and diet can help relieve symptoms of premenstrual syndrome and other causes of menstrual discomfort. Includes a nutrient guide for adult women.
Soft Cover   *160 pages*   *Illustrated*   *$5.95*

GETTING HIGH IN NATURAL WAYS An Infobook for Young People of All Ages
by Nancy Levinson and Joanne Rocklin
Being high is a natural state — and we don't need drugs to get there. A vitally important book for our times.
Soft Cover   *112 pages*   *$6.95*

HELPING YOUR CHILD SUCCEED AFTER DIVORCE by Florence Bienenfeld, Ph.D.
A guide for divorcing parents who want — and need — to make this time as safe as possible for their children.
Soft Cover   *224 pages*   *Illustrated*   *$9.95*

MENOPAUSE WITHOUT MEDICINE by Linda Ojeda, Ph.D.
Preparing for a healthy menopause can never begin too early. Ojeda's natural approach focuses on nutrition, physical conditioning, beauty care, and psychological health.
Hard Cover   *320 pages*   *Illustrated*   *$17.95*   *(Fall, 1988*)*

NOT ANOTHER DIET BOOK: A Right Brain Program for Successful Weight Management
by Bobbe Sommer, Ph.D.
Right brain techniques to gain control of your weight, your self-image, and your life. Includes a six-week program to obtain and maintain the desired weight.
Hard Cover   *256 pages*   *Illustrated*   *$15.95*

NUTRITION AND YOUR BODY by Benjamin Colimore, Ph.D. and Sarah Colimore
Comprehensive and easily read information on how nutrients work in the body and why we need them; with practical advice, recipes, meal planners, and tips that make the difference.
Soft Cover   *260 pages*   *Illustrated*   *$9.95*

ONCE A MONTH: The Original Premenstrual Syndrome Handbook
by Katharina Dalton, M.D.
The first book—and still the best—to explain clearly the symptoms, effects and complete treatment of Premenstrual Syndrome. By the acknowledged pioneer in the field.
Soft Cover   *256 pages*   *Illustrated*   *3rd Edition*   *$8.45*

P·M·S: PREMENSTRUAL SYNDROME A Guide for Young Women by Gilda Berger
The first need is proper information, and this book will help young women through their encounters with PMS.
Soft Cover   *96 pages*   *2nd Edition*   *$6.95*

RAISING EACH OTHER A Book for Teens and Parents
by Jeanne Brondino and the Parent/Teen Book Group.
Honest talk from both generations about freedom, privacy, trust, responsibility, drugs, drinking, sex, other vital issues.
Soft Cover   *160 pages*   *Illustrated*   *$7.95*

*These books may be ordered and paid for in advance; they will be shipped when specified.
Prices Subject to Change Without Notice
See Over for Ordering and Discounts

Add postage and handling at $2.00 for one book and $0.50 for every additional book. Canadian orders: $3.00 first book, $.50 each additional. Please allow 6 to 8 weeks for delivery.

Name _____

Street/Number _____

City/State _____ Zip _____

PLEASE SEND ME:

CHARTING YOUR WAY	_____	@	$2.95 _____
EXCLUSIVELY FEMALE	_____	@	$5.95 _____
GETTING HIGH IN NATURAL WAYS	_____	@	$6.95 _____
HELPING YOUR CHILD SUCCEED	_____	@	$9.95 _____
MENOPAUSE WITHOUT MEDICINE	_____	@	$17.95 _____
NOT ANOTHER DIET BOOK	_____	@	$15.95 _____
NUTRITION AND YOUR BODY	_____	@	$9.95 _____
ONCE A MONTH	_____	@	$8.45 _____
PMS: A GUIDE FOR YOUNG WOMEN	_____	@	$6.95 _____
RAISING EACH OTHER	_____	@	$7.95 _____

TOTAL		$_____
DISCOUNT AT _____ %	**LESS**	$(_____
TOTAL COST OF BOOKS		$_____
Shipping & Handling		$_____
California Residents add Sales Tax		$_____
TOTAL AMOUNT ENCLOSED		$_____

( ) Cash   ( ) Check
( ) Check here to receive our catalog of books

Please complete and mail to:
HUNTER HOUSE INC., PUBLISHERS
PO Box 847, Claremont, CA 91711, USA

If you don't use this offer—give it to a friend!